Casebook to accompany

Shopper, Buyer, and Consumer Behavior

Casebook to accompany
Shopper, Buyer, and Consumer Behavior:
Theory, Marketing Applications, and Public Policy Implications

Second Edition

Dana-Nicoleta Lascu
University of Richmond

Jay D. Lindquist
Western Michigan University

M. Joseph Sirgy
Virginia Polytechnic Institute and State University

Cincinnati, OH
www.atomicdog.com

ISBN 1-59260-067-0

Printed in the United States of America by Atomic Dog Publishing, 1148 Main Street, Third Floor, Cincinnati, OH 45202

10 9 8 7 6 5 4 3 2 1

To Lucia and Damian Lascu
—Dana-Nicoleta Lascu

To my wife, Shirley, and my three children,
Scott, Matthew, and Tiffany
—Jay D. Lindquist

To my wife, Pamela, and my four daughters,
Melissa, Danielle, Michelle, and Emmaline
—M. Joseph Sirgy

Brief Contents

Contents

Preface

Preface

This casebook is designed to help students apply the many concepts and models of consumer behavior using real world examples. The cases involve mostly popular firms dealing with particular problems or opportunities that have consumer behavior implications. Each case has relevance to concepts and models involving several chapters from the textbook. For example, the case involving BMW is relevant to concepts and models described in chapters 1, 3, 6, 7, 12, 14, and 15. The discussion questions at the end of each case help students make the connection between the case and concepts/models described in the textbook. To help students make a connection between the cases and the textbook, we developed a matrix showing where these connections occur (see matrix on the next page).

Shopper, Buyer, and Consumer Behavior Chapters

Cases	Ch1	Ch2	Ch3	Ch4	Ch5	Ch6	Ch7	Ch8	Ch9	Ch10	Ch11	Ch12	Ch13	Ch14	Ch15	Ch16	Ch17	Ch18
A. Ben & Jerry's, Eco-activism, and the Bush Administration										X						X	X	
B. Bavarian Motor Works	X		X			X	X					X		.X	X			
C. Campina, Naturally	X	X	X		X	X						X	X	X				
D. Royal Philips Electronics	X		X						X	X								
E. Hilton Sorrento Palace	X	X	X	X		X	X			X				X				
F. AvtoVAZ	X	X	X									X						
G. Disneyland Resort Paris	X	X	X			X		X		X		X			X			
H. So, Who's the Target Market Here						X							X	X				
I. Enhancing the Quality of Life of the Elderly			X							X								X
J. The Diffusion of E-mail in Health Care										X								X
K. Streaming Media Is Catching On										X			X					X
L. Consumer Trends												X						
M. Demographic Trends												X						
N. Family Values										X	X	X					X	
O. Socially Responsible Consumers or Green Consumers										X							X	
P. I Am Proud to Be American											X	X	X					
Q. Video-on-Demand										X								X

Case

A

Ben & Jerry's, Eco-activism, and the Bush Administration

M. Joseph Sirgy

A-1 Ben & Jerry's, Eco-activism, and the Bush Administration

Ben & Jerry's Homemade, Inc. has an image of being independent, earthy, and hippie like, an image ascribable to the company's founders, Ben Cohen and Jerry Greenfield. Over the years, Ben and Jerry made their brand of ice cream stand out by developing goofy flavor names (occasionally linked to their favorite musicians such as Jerry Garcia and Phish) and their stance on the environment. Now the company has been sold to Unilever, but the environmentalism cause remains linked with the brand name. For example, the most recent cause-related tie-in has been the Dave Matthews Band. Matthews has put his own "green" philosophy on the new flavor, One Sweet Whirled, a play off his song "One Sweet World." The promotion campaign encourages the reduction of greenhouse gases. Marketers at Ben & Jerry have held One Sweet World Interactive Events at Matthews' concert venues, offering tastes of the new product and giving information about how to help reduce global warming. The same information can be found on their website (www.onesweetwhirled.com). At the retail level, Ben & Jerry is setting up "action stations" to encourage people to become active in the environmentalism movement. Portion of the sales go to a consortium called Save Our Environment, to green non-government organizations (NGOs) such as the Sierra Club (www.sierraclub.org), and to the World Wildlife Federation (www.wwf.org). To know more about the consortium, visit their website at www.SaveOurEnvironment.org.

Who buys Ben & Jerry's One Sweet Whirled brand of ice cream? Most young adults and the Baby Boomers! This ice cream is essentially flavored with caramel, coffee, and marshmallow. American Demographics (www.demographics.com) reporter, Matthew Grimm, believes that Ben & Jerry's environmentalism campaign is not making much of a dent because the message is not reach mainstream America (Grimm 2002[1]). He reports the results of a survey of the Gallup organization that tracked American consciousness of global warming. The survey results indicated consciousness of global warming have raised from a low of 24 percent in 1997 to a high of 40 percent in 2000, but then fell to 29 percent in 2002. September 11 and the economic recession have made environmental issues still a lower priority in 2003.

It seems that Ben & Jerry is countering the Bush Administration stance on the environment. The Bush Administration has failed to sign the Koyoto Treaty that puts pressure on governments to take measures to reduce toxic gas emissions. The same administration also has pushed hard to open the Alaskan National Wildlife Refuge to oil drilling despite the fact that the majority of Americans wants a cleaner and safer environment. According to Gallup, 60 percent of Americans favor energy conservation, 72 percent support tougher auto emissions standards, 83 percent favor higher standards for corporate pollution, and 82 percent want tougher enforcement of environmental laws (reported in Grimm 2002).

Grimm also reports that Ben & Jerry has claimed that the company is implementing what they preach to others. The company is evaluating its refrigeration systems to reduce CO_2 emissions; they are looking at alternative energy sources; and they encourage their own employees to buy and consume products in ways that can reduce CO_2 emissions.

Discussion Questions
Discussion Questions

1. One of the important consumer rights is the right to a healthful environment. Ben & Jerry is a company that advocates sustainable consumption. How does it do this? Read the section on Consumer Rights in Chapter 16 and discuss.

2. Do you believe that business should be involved in advocating causes like sustainable consumption? How do you feel about cause-related marketing in general? Read chapters 16 and 17 and discuss.

3. Do you believe that Ben & Jerry's cause-related marketing campaign is successful? Evaluate the campaign using the principles specified in the Communication and Persuasion chapter (Chapter 10).

Note

1. Grimm, Matthews (2002). "Earthy Crunch," *American Demographics* (June), pp. 46–47.

Bavarian Motor Works:
Diversifying a Prestige Brand

Matt Crumley, Dana Lascu, Lisa Myers,
Pascal Ontijd, Taylor Roberts, Kerrie Robinson,
and Sean Wygovsky

Bavarian Motor Works (BMW) is a leading global manufacturer of luxury automobiles. A high-priced, high-performance automobile, the BMW has long been a status product for consumers worldwide. The "Beemer" for consumers in the United States, the "BMW" (pronounced *Beh Em Veh*) for most consumers in continental Europe, this automobile is a legend of style and class. One of BMW's greatest challenges is retaining its leadership position in the luxury automobile market—a challenge that has been recently compounded by the company's decision to diversify into the lower-priced automobile market. Recently, in one of its most daring moves, BMW successfully launched the MINI—a very non–BMW-like automobile, the progeny of BMW's ill-fated relationship with the British Rover group, known as the most beloved British car.

B-1 The Automobile Industry

The boom in the global economy in the late 1990s, coupled with increased consumer confidence, led to high growth in the automobile industry. Vehicle manufacturers were under pressure as never before to increase production, and the globalization of the industry posed further challenges with long-term structural changes for the industry:

1. Mergers and other strategic alliances led to a diminishing pool of independent manufacturers left in the industry.[1] Ford and DaimlerChrysler are likely to acquire additional companies, leading to the projection that by 2005, there will be fewer than ten international players in the automobile market.[2]
2. The Internet is also changing many aspects of the automobile industry. Consumers increasingly use it to research features, specifications, styles, and designs of numerous makes and models. Most importantly, consumers can use independent sources to precisely assess dealer profit and bargain successfully on price, adding to the downward pressure on price the industry is experiencing. In addition, many web sites offer detailed information about specific models, and it is predicted that consumers will be able to circumvent dealerships and order automobiles from manufacturers via the Internet.[3] According to J.D. Power and Associates, 62 percent of new automobile buyers surveyed in 2001 in the United States logged on to the Internet for information on their prospective purchases.[4]
3. Another structural change in the industry is attributed to the evolving technology. The industry has seen substantial growth in "telematics"—the technologies that keep drivers connected to electronic networks.[5]
4. Finally, there is a rising trend of automakers establishing a niche in the marketplace. These automakers are relying on new categories of vehicles that will expand the overall market. Chrysler's new design, the PT Cruiser sedan, has proven to be especially popular, with demand exceeding supply.[6]

In the United States alone, sales of new cars and light trucks reached a record level of 17.4 million units in 2000—an increase of 500,000 units over the previous year's sales of 16.9 million automobiles.[7] The U.S. automobile market is the largest in the world for passenger vehicles.[8] However, with the downturn of the economy in 2001, sales volume fell 2.5 percent, to 16.92 million vehicles.[9] Globally, sales of new vehicles worldwide have also been projected to grow from 50.6 million units in 1998 to 57.2 million in 2005.[10] In Europe, automobile sales for 2001 surpassed the 14.7 million units recorded in 2000.[11]

Karl Rapp created BMW in 1913 as an aircraft engine design shop just outside Munich, the capital of the state of Bavaria, Germany. The name of the shop was Bayerische Motoren Werke (Bavarian Motor Works). At the end of World War I, German aircraft production declined drastically, and the company began producing railway brakes. BMW made its first motorcycle in 1923, and the company began making automobiles in 1928 after purchasing a small automobile manufacturing company. Larger automobiles were added to the product line in 1933 and, in 1941, the company stopped automobile production to produce aircraft for the German air force. Following World War II, the production of automobiles and motorcycles resumed. Over the remainder of the decade, the company expanded through acquisitions and, in 1986, it began producing luxury vehicles. Sales rose and, in 1992, BMW outsold Mercedes in Europe for the first time ever.[12]

Currently, the BMW headquarters constitute a Munich landmark, reigning in its imposing three-cylinder building just outside the Middle Ring (the Middle Beltway) as the city's tallest structure.

BMW Group products are currently in greater demand worldwide than ever before. The fiscal year for 2000 held the record for deliveries, sales, and profits, with net income recorded at $966.1 million.[13] BMW pursues a premium brand strategy and concentrates on markets with above-average growth potential and high margins; with this strategy, BMW sales rose an additional 7 percent in 2001, and sales are expected to grow at a faster pace than the overall market because consumers who typically purchase luxury cars are not affected as much by recession.[14]

B-2 The Company

BMW developed the Herbert Quandt Foundation to promote the company's social involvement. The Herbert Quandt Foundation fosters national and international dialogue and mutual understanding between business, politics, and society. In addition, the foundation organizes a range of important events to bring together the leaders of industry and society. BMW focuses on environmental sustainability, understanding that oil is a limited resource and other forms of energy need to be explored. BMW is currently introducing a new 7 Series powered by hydrogen, and uses much research and development to explore solar-powered alternatives. But BMW's social consciousness goes beyond the environment. In addition to just traffic safety, BMW focuses on social development issues such as intercultural learning, sponsorship of gifted students, and other educational programs.[15]

In addition to its foundation, BMW spreads the word of its excellence in other forums. It is present at the North American International Auto Show in Detroit and the Frankfurt Auto Show. It also sponsors the BMW International Open, one of the most important golf tournaments; the BMW Golf Cup International; and it is present in the Formula 1 Racing circuit.

BMW has national web sites in Austria, Belgium, Czech Republic, Denmark, Ireland, Estonia, Finland, France, Germany, Greece, Great Britain, Hungary, Italy, Lithuania, Netherlands, Norway, Portugal, Russia, Sweden, Switzerland, Spain, and the Ukraine. Also, it covers nineteen countries in the Americas, three in the Middle East, nine in Asia, and in South Africa, Australia, and New Zealand. Its web site offers insights into its long-standing tradition of innovation and quality. Its site, www.bmwfilms.com, offers a display of quality in the form of five different short films with action-packed mini plots. Its automobiles are placed in James Bond movies, and its "Ultimate Driving" message is widely known.

B-3 Communicating Excellence at BMW

BMW offers zero-percent financing and reasonable leasing structures to penetrate the lower income market. Also, it prides itself on continuous customer service with credit, personal banking, credit cards, and insurance.[16] BMW also offers a protection plan, certification, and roadside assistance on all new and used BMW automobiles for most consumers in developed countries. Finally, BMW facilitates buying by offering a program that allows the buyer to customize his or her own car on the web site and have it delivered without even leaving home.

B-4 The BMW Driver

Although BMW has many different types of consumers, a certain type tends to purchase its vehicles: upper middle class and upper class professional males. BMW has recently seen an increase in its female customers.[17] Baby boomers are the primary consumers, as they tend to have the most money to spend. In fact, consumers in this group aged 35–44 account for more new vehicle sales dollars than any other group.[18] Over the years, BMW has sought to target young professionals who are well-educated, college graduates.[19] Recently, however, BMW has widened its target market. It now caters to single, male executives, to families with children, and to older couples.[20] Also, with the addition of the 3 Series, it is attempting to attract the "20-something" generation.

BMW's superior design and quality attract consumers who are very safety conscious, but who are also seeking the status of owning a BMW. BMW's sleek styling also attracts consumers who are style conscious. With the introduction of the 3 Series, a more affordable automobile, BMW has seen a decrease in the average age of its consumers.[21]

B-5 All Things BMW

The company offers a full line of automobiles for a large variety of luxury market segments: It produces sports cars, family cars, performance machines, and a variety of non-car products. BMW's introductory automobile is a BMW 3 Series. The company has a 5 Series targeted at the mid-luxury market and offers a 7 Series for the high-end luxury automobile buyer. BMW also offers sports cars, SUVs, and other vehicles.

The 3 Series BMW, its introductory automobile, is offered as a sedan, coupe, convertible, touring car, and a compact, with 4–8 cylinders and a choice of gas or diesel. Safety is also a key concern in any BMW car, and the 3 Series BMWs have a variety of safety features: special headlight adjustments, multiple airbags, and special braking systems.[22] Manufacturer's Suggested Retail Price (MSRP) for these cars ranges from $27,100 to $42,400.[23] A typical 3 Series BMW could be considered a 325 Series four-door vehicle. The price tag of this car usually runs $27,100. The BMW has as standard features a 2.5L, 6-cylinder, and 184-horsepower engine with a 5-speed transmission, ABS brakes, front and rear antiroll bars, a multilink suspension, rack and pinion steering, front- and rear-vented brakes, sixteen-inch alloy rims, and a full-size spare. Standard safety features include side impact bars, driving lights, a full gauge panel, multiple airbags, and a security system.[24]

The BMW 5 Series is its mid-price offering. A sedan and a touring car are the options available in the 5 Series. These vehicles are also offered in a 4-cylinder engine with a choice of fuel consumption. Safety and design are enhanced for this series. The sophisticated safety system includes crumple zones, airbags, and tire pressure controls, among others.[25] MSRP ranges from $35,950 to $39,450.[26]

The top of the line BMW is the 7 Series. This high-end vehicle is available in an 8-cylinder, 6-speed transmission. Safety and the ultimate in luxury are the key components in this vehicle. The car comes with a very sophisticated safety system that utilizes fourteen sensors to maintain safety and comfort.[27] MSRP for this automobile ranges from $67,850 to $71,850.[28]

BMW also offers a variety of additional vehicles such as sports cars and sports utility vehicles (SUVs). The BMW Z3 is its sports car. The automobile is available in a coupe or roadster with a 4- or 6-cylinder engine. Safety features include impact safety absorbers, electronic ignition immobilizer, and smart airbags.[29] MSRP ranges from $31,300 to $37,900 for this BMW.[30] The X5 is the BMW performance SUV, available in the normal X5 and the X5 4.6is. The normal X5 comes with a 6-cylinder engine, while the X5 4.6 is available with a powerful 8-cylinder engine. Safety features include a high-impact body shell, head and side airbags, and a sophisticated braking system.[31] The MSRP ranges from $38,900 to $66,200.[32] The BMW Z8 is the ultimate in driving performance, offering the highest quality and performance of any of BMW's products. The car comes with an electronic-start 8-cylinder engine that is completely electronically controlled. This BMW is a high-performance computer-run car.[33] The MSRP for this car is around $130,000.[34]

BMW also produces M Series stock vehicles with "muscle" as the main function. These high-performance machines are made especially for those individuals searching for very high performance, safety, and design. Suspension, wheels, brakes, exhaust, and engine components are all modified to increase performance to its highest level. The M series is available as an M3 coupe, M3 convertible, M5 sedan, M coupe, or an M roadster.[35] MSRP for these driving machines range from $44,900 to $69,990.[36]

BMW also has an array of other products in an attempt to decrease the cyclical aspect of automobile retailing and increase diversification. BMW offers eleven different types of motorcycles that are used for a variety of purposes: touring, racing, street, and off-road use. Prices range from $8,000 upward to $30,000. BMW also offers a full line of motorcycle and car apparel and accessories. Clothes, bikes, and other similar products are all offered by the company.[37]

The automobile manufacturer also offers financial services, BMW driver training, BMW international Direct and Corporate Sales, BMW ASSIST, and sponsorships. The company makes information available such as split-screen maps, digital road maps, and drivers' assistance programs. BMW also produces a C1, similar to a covered motorcycle, which is used in crowded cities to move in tight places. It is also involved in the comeback of the MINI as it reaches for world markets.[38]

B-6 Competition within the Luxury Automobile Segment

According to numerous web sites quoting *Consumer Reports*,[39] a comparison between luxury automobiles with prices between $40,000 to $60,000 reveals that the BMW 5 Series lives up to the slogan "the ultimate driving machine," and it is spacious, comfortable, responsive, powerful, and safe, yet its options are very expensive. In comparison, the Mercedes E class is more fuel efficient than the BMW; it is large, comfortable, among the safest in the automobile industry; and it handles well but not in snow. The Lexus GS is also more fuel efficient than the BMW; it is comfortable, reliable, and quite luxurious; and it fits its slogan "Passionate pursuit of perfection." It has rear-wheel drive, which needs getting used to, and its options are also expensive.

For automobiles with a price range from $30,000 to $40,000, the BMW 3 Series is very responsive; it accelerates quickly and breaks well, has smooth steering, but also has rear-wheel drive, which may pose a challenge; and it is quite loud. The Mercedes C class is less fuel efficient, but it provides a safe and quiet ride. The Lexus ES has a firm front-wheel drive; it is luxurious, spacious, and reliable, but its extra options are expensive.

In terms of market performance, BMW's sales rose 15 percent through November 2001, vaulting it into second place among luxury automobiles in the United States. BMW sales jumped over Mercedes-Benz, which now holds the third spot. Mercedes-Benz has been slumping since 1998, when the company completed its merger with Chrysler, forming DaimlerChrysler. Toyota Motor Corporation's Lexus currently holds the number-one slot in the U.S. market.[40] There is fierce competition among the luxury automobile makers, and focusing on such factors as customer service, price, and new product innovations will help BMW outperform its competitors.

B-7 Targeting to Lower-Price Segments: The MINI and the Certified Pre-Owned BMWs

B-7a A Truly Unique Car: "The MINI puts a smile on your face."

With the March 2002 introduction of the MINI to the United States, BMW hopes to gain a share of the small and compact car market. Targeting a high-tech and high-style consumer, the MINI features heated mirrors, a computer navigation system, an air-conditioned glove box, rain-sensing windshield wipers, and an eight-speaker premium stereo.[41] The very "Euro-looking" MINI also features bright, flashy colors and a hard top that is of a different color. The wide range of colors and options gives each owner the opportunity to personalize it.

The BMW Group's 2000 Annual Report states, "Through the MINI brand, the BMW Group will further enhance its appeal to young and modern customers. With its emotional character, the MINI is tailored precisely to these target groups and meets the growing demand for premium offers also in the small car segment."[42] The MINI has fared well in Europe. The drivers, typically young, urban, and trendy, find the MINI easy to drive and park in congested cities and appreciate the high kilometer to gasoline liter ratio.[43] The MINI is quite small, under 12 feet long, and 4 feet 7 inches tall; with its doors open, it is wider than it is long.[44] BMW hopes to lure the same segment that Volkswagen did so successfully with its new Beetle.[45]

BMW hopes not only to woo new customers, but also to bring back current owners of the larger BMW cars. "The MINI will give BMW Group an excellent position in the small car segment in the future, especially as a MINI is the ideal second or third car for the BMW driver and other customers in existing BMW segments."[46] The price is right for many consumers at $16,850 to $19,850, less than half the price of a BMW.[47]

BMW sells the MINI through MINI franchises, which do not carry the BMW name; any dealers that are approved to carry the MINI have to provide separate facilities for the automobiles.[48] In addition, the car itself will not show the BMW logo but will have a separate MINI logo.

B-7b Problems with the MINI

In an effort to reach bargain-conscious consumers, BMW provides the MINI at an exceptionally low price. Serious concerns have been raised about the quality of the MINI and the fact that it is associated with the BMW name. Brand name dilution may be a serious future concern. BMW owners typically desire luxury and status; however, with the MINI being so price competitive, it is possible that many who cannot afford to purchase a BMW will purchase a MINI to be a part of the BMW family of cars. On the other hand, "as a luxury brand, if you lower your price range, it gets more risky," says Wendelin Wiedeking, president and chief executive of Porsche AG. "Exclusivity is very much related to price."[49]

More problems with the MINI have arisen in the company's international markets. A recall of 500 MINIs took place after workers noticed sparks while fueling vehicles.[50] More than 6,500 vehicles were retrofitted in order to correct the problem, costing BMW more than $508,000.[51] These types of setbacks have the potential to inflict damage to a prestigious brand name. "People are watching the MINI launch very carefully," said John Lawson, an analyst at Schroder Salomon Smith Barney. "They need to be convinced that the MINI will be a high-quality product and will be sensitive to anything that suggests it is not."[52]

BMW has focused its advertising efforts on its Certified Pre-Owned vehicles in 2002. The Certified Pre-Owned BMW is given a warranty and a series of checks in order to be classified as Certified. With this new push toward selling used cars, BMW might again be risking a dilution of brand image with luxury-conscious consumers. Making the BMW name a more affordable prospect to more segments of the population may reduce the prestige and luxury appeal of a BMW. In addition, continuous advertising of a pre-owned vehicle can lessen the brand name in the eyes of prestige-conscious consumers.

B-7c The Certified Pre-Owned BMWs

Discussion Questions

1. As you analyze this case, focus on segmentation and the targeting strategy used by BMW in marketing the MINI and the Certified Pre-Owned BMW.
2. How is the BMW positioned in the consumer's mind? Describe the typical BMW driver, using psychographic and demographic variables for the description. What leisure activities does this driver engage in? What are the driver's hobbies? What magazines does the driver subscribe to?
3. What strategy suggestions would you offer to BMW to ensure that the MINI and the Certified Pre-Owned BMW do not dilute the BMW brand?

Notes

1. "Worldwide Automotive Database and Forecasts," *Motor Business International,* London, Second Quarter 2000, pp. 165–271.
2. "Passenger Cars, ATVs, RVs and Pick-ups in the USA (July 2001)," www.euromonitor.com.
3. Ibid.
4. "Autos & Auto Parts Industry Survey," *Standard & Poor's,* December 27, 2001.
5. Ibid.
6. Ibid.
7. "Passenger Cars, ATVs, RVs and Pick-ups in the USA (July 2001)," www.euromonitor.com.
8. "Autos & Auto Parts Industry Survey," *Standard & Poor's,* December 27, 2001.
9. Ibid.
10. "World Vehicle Industry Prospects to 2005," *Motor Business International,* London, Third Quarter 1999, pp. 88–100.
11. Michael Robinet, "The Mixed Scene in Europe," *Automotive Design & Production,* Cincinnati, February 2002, Vol. 114, No. 2, pp. 24–25.
12. www.hoovers.com
13. Ibid.
14. Beth Reigber, "Companies: BMW Says Sales . . ." *The Wall Street Journal Europe,* January 29, 2002.
15. More information about the Herbert Quandt Foundation can be found at www.herbertquandtstiftung.com.
16. A complete list of financial services can be found at http://www.bmw-financialservices.com/international/index.html.
17. "Passenger Cars, ATVs, RVs and Pick-ups in the USA (July 2001)," www.euromonitor.com.
18. Ibid.
19. "BMW" Encyclopedia of Major Marketing Campaigns.
20. Ibid.
21. "Passenger Cars, ATVs, RVs and Pick-ups in the USA (July 2001)" www.euromonitor.com.
22. www.carsDirect.com, Research Center, February 25, 2002.
23. www.bmw.com, Products, February 25, 2002.
24. www.carsDirect.com, Compare Vehicles, February 25,2002.
25. www.bmw.com, Products, February 25, 2002.
26. www.carsDirect.com, Research Center, February 25, 2002.
27. www.bmw.com, Products, February 25, 2002.
28. www.carsDirect.com, Research Center, February 25, 2002.
29. www.bmw.com, Products, February 25, 2002.
30. www.carsDirect.com, Research Center, February 25, 2002.
31. www.bmw.com, Products, February 25, 2002.
32. www.carsDirect.com, Research Center, February 25, 2002.
33. www.bmw.com, Products, February 25, 2002.
34. www.carsDirect.com, Research Center, February 25, 2002.
35. www.bmw.com, Products, February 25, 2002.
36. www.carsDirect.com, Research Center, February 25, 2002.
37. www.bmw.com, Products, February 25, 2002.
38. Ibid.
39. Information is taken from the following web pages: www.epinions.com; www.caranddriver.com; www.newcartestdrive.com; www.auto.com; www.edmunds.com and www.autoweb.com.
40. Bill Koenig and Jeff Green, "High-end Cars . . .," *National Post,* December 11, 2001.
41. Gregory White, "High Style in a Tiny Package . . .," *The Wall Street Journal,* October 17, 2001.
42. BMW Group AG, 2000 Annual Report.
43. White, "High Style in a Tiny Package . . .," October 17, 2001.

44. Ibid.

45. Terry Box, "Got Your Eye on a MINI?..." *The Dallas Morning News,* January 26, 2002.

46. BMW Group AG, 2000 Annual Report.

47. Box, "Got Your Eye on a MINI?..." January 26, 2002.

48. Ibid.

49. White, "High Style in a Tiny Package . . .," October 17, 2001.

50. Suzanne Kapner, "BMW Faces Setback with Its Entry into Small Car Market," *The New York Times,* September 4, 2001.

51. Ibid.

52. Ibid.

Campina, Naturally[1]

Dana Lascu

Campina is one of the leading dairy companies in the world and one of the few that produces only dairy products. A European company that remains close to its Dutch roots, Campina's image evokes picturesque Dutch cow pastures and healthy lifestyles. The company's history can be traced to Southern Holland, in the Eindhoven area; a dairy cooperative with the name "De Kempen" was created in 1947 and used the brand name "Campina." In 1964 the cooperative merged with another cooperative in the Weert region in Holland and formed Campina (named after a regional moor—its meaning is "from the land"). After several consecutive mergers—more recently, with Melkunie Holland—Campina Melkunie (or Campina, as it is informally known) became the largest dairy cooperative in the Netherlands.

In the Netherlands alone, Campina boasts 7,500 member dairy farmers. The farmers own the cooperative: Campina must buy all the milk the farmers produce, while the farmers must finance the cooperative and, in return, they obtain a yield of the products sold. Campina itself is a nonprofit organization. Member farmers receive all the company profits. They have voting rights in the company that are proportional to the amount of milk they deliver, and they are represented by the Members' Council, the highest managerial body of the cooperative.

The separation between Campina, the operating company, and its cooperatives is evident: Campina is headquartered in Zaltbommel, in an industrial park in Southern Holland, while the dairies are located close to the consumers they serve, in different areas of the country.

C-1 Industry Trends

Among the main trends in the international dairy industry are the following:

Consolidation is a dominant trend of the dairy industry. The number of dairy companies is falling, and the production capacity of those that remain is increasing and becoming more efficient.[2] Yet there are still companies that exist successfully in the $100 million to $200 million range of sales, surviving through a mix of ingenuity and innovation.[3]

The European Union remains the world's top dairy producer, manufacturer, and trader of dairy products; because the EU is a mature dairy market, the emphasis is on value growth and processing milk into products with high added value.[4] As such, Campina's strategy and general mission, "adding value to milk," fits well with this trend. Of the world's top twenty-five dairy organizations, fourteen have their headquarters in Europe.[5]

The degree of concentration varies significantly, however, from region to region. In Scandinavia and the Netherlands, a handful of major cooperatives dominate. In Greece, there are more than 1,000 dairy businesses, of which more than 700 make cheese. In Germany, the industry has changed from numerous small, localized firms to most milk processors either collapsing or merging. In France, the top five control 55 percent of milk production. And in Scandinavia, the major players wield even more control: in Denmark, MD Foods and Klover Maelk control 95 percent of milk production, and in Sweden, Arla handles 80 percent.[6]

Another important trend is the focus on convenience (a packaging issue) and on value-added nutrition for functional foods (a product ingredient issue). Changes include creating new packaging and unique containers for innovative products. For example, German-based Schwalbchen Molkerei has debuted Go! Banana, the first milk-energy drink made from fresh milk and real, pureed bananas, packaged in 330 ml Tetra Prisma cartons with fluted sides. Spain's Pascual Dairy offers milk-based energy drink Bio Frutas in two flavors: Tropical and Mediterranean. German milk processor Immergut has introduced Drinkfit Choco Plus, a vitamin-fortified, chocolate-flavored milk, in the same carton. The United Kingdom company Miller offers dual-compartment, side-by-side containers of refrigerated yogurt, while a new drinkable fruit yogurt from Nestle SA debuted in the United Kingdom under the name Squizzos, sporting Disney Jungle Book characters in a triangular-shaped package that is easy to tear, squeeze, and drink.[7]

Cheese is also presented in innovative packaging. Baars, a subsidiary of the BolsWessanen Group, a United Kingdom Dutch company, launched a smooth, flavorful medium/mature cheddar cheese, named Maidwell, that does not crumble; it is sold in an attractive, innovative, clear-plastic, resealable pack. Rumblers, a convenient all-in-one breakfast product manufactured by Ennis Foods Ltd., United Kingdom, is also available in an innovative package that holds cereal and fresh, semiskimmed milk separately, all in one pack.[8]

Functional ingredients (health foods or ingredients that enhance the nutritional value of products) represent yet another important trend in the dairy industry: Dairy products represent the most important sector, accounting for 65 percent of sales in a sector that is very buoyant given the consumer interest in health and diet.[9] The leading companies in Europe in this domain are Campina Melkunie (Netherlands), Nestle (Switzerland), and Danone (France).[10] Worldwide, Japan leads in the functional foods trend and is the only country with a regulatory policy on such foods: FOSHU (Foods for Specified Health Use).[11] There is a tradition of lactic acid bacteria culture drinks and yogurts in Japan, and many of these fermented drinks and yogurts contain other functional ingredients, such as oligofructose, calcium, and DHA, which is a polyunsaturated fatty acid derived from fish oil that is said to improve learning, lower blood pressure, help prevent cancer, and lower serum cholesterol.[12] And from Dairy Gold, Australia, comes Vaalia Passionfruit Smoothie, a low-fat milk-based drink containing 25 percent fruit juice, acidophilus and bifidus cultures, and insulin.[13]

C-2 Meeting Competitive Challenges at Campina: Adopting a Market Orientation

Historically, milk production has been supply driven, and excess milk was used to produce cheese and powder milk; this strategy led to excess cheese/commodities on the market and the need for subsidies. Campina initiated a change in this practice. In the past fifteen years, the company has been demand driven: Farmers are assigned production quotas that they are not allowed to exceed.

In other attempts to adopt a market orientation, Campina decided to eliminate all milk powder production because milk powder is a low-margin commodity. Instead, the company is focusing on building the brand to ensure recognition by consumers as a value offering and as a quality brand name.

According to R. J. Steetskamp, Director of Strategic Business Development at Campina, the company examines consumer behavior to determine where to fit Campina products in consumers' lives. As such, Campina offers four categories of products:

1. **Indulgence products.** This category constitutes an important growth area for the company. Campina produces numerous milk-based desserts, with the exception of ice cream—primarily due to the product's seasonality and the logistics strategies involved in the transportation and storage of ice cream, which differ from those for the rest of the company's offerings.
2. **Daily essentials.** This category includes Campina products that shoppers purchase routinely, such as milk, buttermilk, yogurt, coffee cream, butter,

cheese, and others. Campina, using a strategy employed by all its competitors, also sells daily essentials under dealer (store) brands, rather than under its own brand name. For example, in Holland, it sells milk, plain yogurt, butter, Gouda cheese, and vla (chocolate or vanilla custard) under the Albert Heijn brand name. Albert Heijn is a dominant, quality supermarket chain in Holland that is owned by Royal Ahold—a large conglomerate that also owns supermarket chains in the United States (BI-LO, Giant, and Stop & Shop). The company also sells daily essentials under dealer brands in Germany.

3. **Functional products.** According to Mr. Steetskamp, this product category needs to be further explored and defined by the company. In this category are health foods and other milk-based nutritional supplements sold to consumers. DMV International is a Campina division that is present all over the world; it produces pharmaceutical products, food ingredients, and ingredients used to enhance the nutrition of consumers and their pets, such as proteins and powders with different functions. All these products are milk-based, and many of them are well known. For example, Lactoval is a popular calcium supplement.

4. **Ingredients (food and pharmaceutical ingredients).** This product category is targeted at other food product manufacturers, rather than at the individual consumers. The primary purpose of the food and pharmaceutical ingredients is to enhance the quality, taste, texture, and/or nutritive content of the products manufactured by Campina's clients. The company's Creamy Creation unit specializes in blending dairy and alcohol to make various cream liqueurs, leading to both healthy and indulgent drinks. In this category fall meal replacement drinks and high protein drinks as well. With this category, Campina becomes a supplier to other manufacturers, rather than a product manufacturer distributing to supermarkets.

C-3 International Expansion at Campina

One of the most important undertakings at Campina in the last decade was to expand beyond the Netherlands. In its first expansion effort, the company bought Belgium's Comelco, another dairy cooperative. In Belgium, the company boasts the Joyvalle dairy products and milk brand and the Passendale, Père Joseph, and Wynendale cheese brands, all marketed under the Campina umbrella brand.

Campina expanded into Germany, purchasing a number of cooperatives: Sudmilch (Southern Germany), Tuffi (Western Germany), and Emzett (Berlin). In Germany, its primary brand is Landliebe; here, the company sells Landliebe milk, cream, yogurts (seasonal, fruit, plain, and in different types of containers); different types of puddings including rice pudding, ice cream, cheese, and qwark (a traditional creamy cheese) plain or with fruit; yogurt drinks (with fruit flavors such as banana, cherry, lemon, peach, and orange); and different milk drinks with flavors such as vanilla and chocolate. The company also offers products such as coffee machines, cups, spoons, and others for purchase online at its site, www.landliebe-online.de. According to R. J. Steetskamp, the Campina name will be used as the umbrella brand for all the company products; the name comes from the Latin "from the land," and it is easily pronounced in all the different languages in Europe, the brand's target market. The only brands that will not be brought under the Campina umbrella brands, according to Mr. Steetskamp, are the Mona brand in the Netherlands and the Landliebe brand in Germany because both have high brand franchise with consumers in their respective countries. Interestingly, the Landliebe brand name is close in meaning to Campina, both making reference to the land.

As a result of these acquisitions and mergers, according to Mr. Steetskamp, Campina is the market leader in Holland, Germany, and Belgium—as the company web site states, "Campina is a household name in the Netherlands, Belgium and Germany."[14]

Campina has further expanded, with its own subsidiaries in the United Kingdom, Spain, Poland, and Russia, where it ultimately plans to use the Campina brand name (the Campina Fruttis brand is one of the most popular fruit yogurt brands in Russia).

Discussion Questions

1. Perform a product mix analysis for Campina. Calculate product length, width, and line depth and evaluate product consistency across the different lines. Refer to www.campina-melkunie.nl for additional brand information.

2. Attempt a comparison with U.S. dairy strategies: Go to your local grocery store chain and note the different brands of milk. Are indulgence products offered by the same company? (Most likely they are not.) Can you find one dairy cooperative that offers milk, butter, cream cheese, and sour cream? Explain the differences between Campina strategies and U.S. dairy cooperatives' strategies.

Notes

1. Case designed with input from Anne Carson, Todd Fowler, Kim Hribar, Liz Manera, and Brian Thoms.
2. Sarah McRitchie, "Europe Shrinks to Expand," *Dairy Foods,* January 1999, Vol. 100, No. 1, pp. 75–79.
3. Gerry Clark and Dave Fusaro, "Survival of the Smallest," *Dairy Foods,* August 1999, Vol. 100, No. 8, pp. 48–55.
4. Ibid.
5. Ibid.
6. McRitchie, "Europe Shrinks to Expand," pp. 75–79.
7. Ibid.
8. Ibid.
9. Ibid.
10. Ibid.
11. Donna Gorski Berry, "Global Dairy Food Trends," *Dairy Foods,* October 1998, Vol. 99, No. 10, pp. 32–37.
12. Ibid.
13. Ibid.
14. www.campina-melkunie.nl

Royal Philips Electronics

*Christianne Goldman, Ryan Ganley, Dana Lascu,
Leslie Ramich, and Akshay Patil*

Case Outline

D-1 Background

Royal Philips is the world's third-largest consumer electronics firm, following market leaders Matsushita and Sony. The Philips brands include Philips, Norelco, Marantz, and Magnavox. The company was established in 1891 in Eindhoven, in the Southern region of the Netherlands, primarily as a manufacturer of incandescent lamps and other electrical products. The company first produced carbon-filament lamps and, by the turn of the century, it had become one of the largest producers in Europe. Later, the company diversified into many other areas, such as electronics, small appliances, lighting, semiconductors, medical systems, and domestic care products, among others. The company headquarters moved to Amsterdam in the 1980s, but its lighting division continues to occupy the center of Eindhoven.

Around the early 1900s, Philips started to diversify its offerings to radio valves and X-ray equipment, and later to television. Later in the century, Philips developed the electric shaver and invented the rotary heads, which led to the development of the Philipshave electric shaver. Philips also made major contributions in the development of television pictures, its research work leading to the development of the Plumbicon television camera tube, which offered a better picture quality. It introduced the compact audiocassette in 1963 and produced its first integrated circuits in 1965. In the 1970s, its research in lighting contributed to the development of the PL and SL energy-saving lamps. More recent Philips innovations are the LaserVision optical disc, the compact disc, and optical telecommunication systems.[1]

Philips expanded in the 1970s and 1980s, acquiring Magnavox (1974) and Signetics (1975), the television business of GTE Sylvania (1981), and the lamps division of Westinghouse (1983). Currently, Philips operates in more than sixty countries, with more than 186,000 employees, and is market leader in many regions for a number of product categories—for example, lighting, shavers, and LCD displays.[2]

In the 1990s, Philips carried out a major restructuring program and changed from highly localized production to globalized production; this change translated into a more efficient concentration of manufacturing—from more than 100 manufacturing sites to 36, and to 14 sites for production: Juarez and Manaus in Latin America; Bruges, Dreux, and Hasselt in Western Europe; Kwidzyn, Szekesfehervar, and Szombathelv in Eastern Europe; and Beijing, Suhzou, Shenzen, and Chungli (all in China) in Asia.

Another important change was the appointment of Gerard Kleisterlee as president of Philips and chairman of the Board of Management in 2001. Kleisterlee has been seen as a Philips man, following a traditional Philips career path that had been embraced by company employees until the 1980s. He was trained locally, at the Eindhoven Technical University, in electronic engineering, and he has worked with the company for three decades. According to Martien Groenewegen, former research and development engineer with Philips, Kleisterlee is perceived by present and former employees as taking the company back to its original path to success. In fact, in a recent interview, Kleisterlee mentioned that the company is presently concentrating on its initial core activities with a focus on its key areas of profitability; this is a different type of restructuring from earlier attempts, when the company pursued "wrong activities."[3] Mr. Groenewegen contends that the perception among employees and the industry is that Philips, under Kleisterlee's leadership, will have a strong product orientation and that it would support an environment in which product innovation will constitute a primary focus of the company. That has been, historically, Philips' proven path to success.

Philips offers consumer products, such as communications products (cordless phones, mobile phones, fax machines), electronics (Flat TV, Real Flat TV, digital TV, projection TV, professional TV, DVD players and recorders, Super Audio CD, VCRs, satellite receivers, CD recorders/players, home theater systems, Internet audio players, shelf systems, portable radios, clock radios, PC monitors, multimedia projectors, PC cameras, PC audio, CD rewriteable drives, DVD drives, among others); home and body care products (vacuum cleaners, irons, kitchen appliances, shavers, oral healthcare products), and lighting products. Its professional products include connectivity, lighting, medical systems (such as magnetic resonance imaging, ultrasound equipment, X-rays), semiconductors, and other products, such as security systems, manufacturing technologies, automotive products, broadband networks, and so on.

D-2 Philips' Offerings

Among Philips' competitors are Matsushita, Sony, Hitachi, and Thomson. Matsushita Electric Industrial is the world's number-one consumer electronics firm. In North America, Matsushita makes consumer, commercial, and industrial electronics (from jukeboxes to flat-screen TVs) under the Panasonic, Technics, and Quasar brands. Matsushita sells consumer products (which account for 40 percent of sales) such as VCRs, CD and DVD players, TVs, and home appliances. It also sells computers, telephones, industrial equipment (welding and vending machines, medical equipment, car navigation equipment), and components such as batteries, semiconductors, and electric motors. The Matsushita group includes about 320 operating units in more than forty-five countries. Its products are sold worldwide, but Asia accounts for more than 70 percent of sales.[4]

D-3 The Competition

Sony is another competitor whose PlayStation home video game systems account for nearly 10 percent of the company's electronics and entertainment sales. Sony, the world's second-largest consumer electronics firm after Matsushita, also makes several other products, including semiconductors, DVD players, batteries, cameras, MiniDisc and Walkman stereo systems, computer monitors, and flat-screen TVs. The company's TVs, VCRs, stereos, and other consumer electronics account for more than 65 percent of sales. Sony's entertainment assets include Columbia TriStar (movies and television shows) and record labels Columbia and Epic. The company also operates insurance and finance businesses.[5]

Hitachi, another large player in the consumer electronics industry, is a leading manufacturer of both electronics components and industrial equipment. The company manufactures mainframes, semiconductors, workstations, elevators and escalators, power plant equipment, and also metals, wire, and cable. Hitachi produces consumer goods, such as audio and video equipment, refrigerators, and washing machines. Similarly to Philips, Hitachi is focusing on developing Internet-related businesses and expanding its information technology units, which account for more than 30 percent of sales.[6]

Finally, Thomson Multimedia is another major competitor and leading manufacturer of consumer electronics (which account for nearly 80 percent of sales), including TVs, video cameras, telephones, audio products, DVD players, and professional video equipment. Thomson Multimedia also produces displays and TV components. Its products, which are sold in more than 100 countries, include brands such as RCA in the United States and Thomson in Europe. Almost 60 percent of the company's sales are in the U.S.[7]

D-4 Philips' Brand Image

Philips' primary mission is to "continually enhance people's lives through technology and innovation."[8] This philosophy is also reflected in its tagline "Let's make things better," launched in 1995.[9] Philips focuses on the multisensory impact of its products and their power to create memories and spur emotions to touch people's lives on a very personal level; Philips also aspires to be the world's leading eco-efficient company in electronics and lighting.[10]

While Philips is a household name in European markets, the company continues to struggle to spread brand awareness in the United States. As recently as 1996, the Philips brand was virtually unknown in the United States, compared with competitors Sony and RCA; the brand was associated with milk of magnesia, petroleum, or screwdrivers.[11] After spending millions to build brand awareness, Philips has successfully achieved recognition among consumers in the U.S. as a brand that makes exciting products that improve people's lives. In 1998, for example, Philips spent $100 million in advertising, sponsorships, movie tie-ins, and retail promotions worldwide to boost brand awareness.[12] In the same year, Philips embarked on its Star campaign in an attempt to create a more human, imaginative, and seductive brand image. Using dynamic state-of-the-art products, the Philips campaign was able to reach consumers on a very personal level, thus gaining their trust, loyalty, and brand preference. The campaign resonated very well with its target market: well-educated, independent, and carefree consumers.[13]

Another venue for communicating with its target market is Philips' five-year sponsorship of the U.S. Soccer Federation as of June 2001. This sponsorship is also expected to help Philips reach more of its young target consumers and more female consumers. Philips thus has 30-second air spots on ABC and ESPN during soccer broadcasts, as well as a presence on stadium billboards, and logo visibility on all training kits; and the Philips' branded goal cameras are highly visible.[14]

Apart from the need to generate awareness in the U.S. markets, Philips also recognizes the need for consolidation and consistency across all of its marketing communications worldwide. To this end, Philips awarded its $600 million account in media buying and planning to the Aegis Group's Carat International.[15] With Carat's help, Philips is attempting to

- Create a consistent brand experience that will give all products a shared look and feel and will demonstrate a deep understanding of the customer[16]
- Become more consumer-focused and more brand-centric in its marketing efforts, expanding beyond its traditional television and print communications to direct marketing and more unconventional media
- Create a total marketing package, which will resonate well with the U.S. consumer and therefore lead to increased U.S. sales[17]
- Engage in extensive direct marketing and Internet marketing; this is especially possible given Philips' alliance with AOL Time Warner[18]

Discussion Questions

1. Use the standardization versus adaptation arguments to support Philips' strategies worldwide. What are some of the advantages of its new standardization strategy?

2. Some may argue that Philips is a Pan-European brand that is trying to make inroads into the United States. Find support for and against this argument.

3. Offer suggestions to Philips regarding the strategies that it can use to create a unified, resonant global brand.

Notes

1. Material available at www.philips.com.
2. www.philips.com
3. Bill Griffeth, *Philips Electronics—CHM & CEO—Interview,* Dow Jones Business Video, January 9, 2002, p. 1.
4. Hoover's Online, www.hoover.com, February 19, 2002.
5. Ibid.
6. Ibid.
7. Ibid.
8. Jennifer B. Simes, "Philippines a Key Hub, Says Philips," *Computerworld Philippines,* Dow Jones Interactive, December 10, 2001, p. 1.
9. "Brand Building," www.philips.com, p. 1.
10. "A Serious Responsibility," www.philips.com, p. 1.
11. Michael McCarthy, "Philips Can't Lose with Puppies, Beatles," *USA Today,* www.usatoday.com, January 15, 2001, p. 2.
12. Tobi Elkin, "Building a Brand," *Vision Magazine,* www.ce.org/, July/August 1999, pp. 1–2.
13. See "Owning the Right Image," www.news.philips.com, p. 1, for a more extensive analysis of the Philips communication strategy.
14. Tobi Elkin, "Philips to Sponsor U.S. Soccer Games," Adage.com, www.adage.com, June 19, 2001, p. 1.
15. Tobi Elkin and Richard Linnett, "Media Moves Up," *Advertising Age,* ABI Inform, July 9, 2001, p. 2.
16. Message from the President, Annual Report 2001, www.philips.com, p. 2.
17. Elkin and Linnett, "Media Moves Up," p. 3.
18. Philips Mainstream Consumer Electronics Powerpoint presentation, www.philips.com.

Hilton Sorrento Palace:
Changing Targeting Strategies

Dana-Nicoleta Lascu

Two hours south of Rome, to Naples, by the Eurostar, the Italian high-speed train, and an additional hour west along the Bay of Naples via the Circum-vesuviana regional railway is the town of Sorrento. The Hilton Sorrento Palace reigns high on the hills of Sorrento, overlooking Mount Vesuvius, the now dormant volcano (since 1944), which buried the towns of Pompeii and Herculaneum in the year 79 A.D.

Sorrento is a small resort town, known well throughout Europe, an ideal vacation destination for its picturesque location and mild weather. A favorite of British travelers, the town of Sorrento has 10,000 beds according to Mr. Ziad Tantawi, director of business development at the Hilton Sorrento Palace. The Hilton Sorrento Palace is the largest of all hotels in the small resort town, with 383 rooms. Owned by the Sorrento Palace Gruppo, its owner since its year of construction (1981), the hotel became part of the Hilton chain in May 2001, and is now under Hilton management. One of the few hotels open in the winter, the Sorrento Palace boasts an average occupancy rate of 60 percent, with an average occupancy of 30 percent from November to March and more than 85 percent from May to October.[1]

The Hilton Sorrento Palace faces competition from bed and breakfasts. These family-run lodges are very popular because they are competitively priced at or below the room rates of leading hotels in the area. Most bed and breakfast accommodations are open year round. Sorrento is also a popular destination for cruise lines during the summer months. For cruise ship passengers, Sorrento offers easy access to the ruins of Pompeii, Mount Vesuvius, and the Isle of Capri. Overall, prices for cruise ships are higher than that of hotels, but they include meals and entertainment, as well as airfare to Italy.

Other local hotels compete directly with the Sorrento Hilton. The historic Europa Palace Grand Hotel, for example, offers close views of the Bay of Naples and the cliffs of Sorrento.

E-1 The Hotel Offerings

The four-star Hilton Sorrento Palace is situated on a hill overlooking the town and the Bay of Naples, a short walk from downtown's busy tourist markets. Surrounded by residences and lemon and orange groves, the hotel is modern and elegant. Its restaurant L'Argumento is situated amidst blooming cannas and orange and lemon trees. Le Ginestre has frescoes and elegant columns, and an indoor pool with a lush painted background. Its other four restaurants abound in blooming bougainvillea and oleander and have a splendid view of the Bay of Naples and Mount Vesuvius.

The indoor lounge has excellent performers scheduled every evening and boasts a view of the city and the Bay.

The executive lounge is situated on the top floor of the hotel and has a splendid view of the Gulf and town. It also boasts a swimming pool at the highest altitude in the region. The lounge serves complimentary food and drinks to executive guests and to gold- and diamond-level Hilton Honors members.

The hotel has a total of six outdoor swimming pools of different depths, flowing into each other, a tennis court, and a relatively well-equipped fitness center. Among the services offered at the hotel pool are the Hilton Kids Club: Every day, from 10 to 12 and from 2 to 4 in the afternoon, the Hilton kids can enjoy entertainment by the pool (uno spazio giochi per bambini).

The hotel's targeting strategies focus primarily on meetings: Its meeting space is one of the largest in Europe. The Centro Congressi (congress center) has a full range of rooms for conferences and conventions of any type or size, from the 1,700-seat auditorium to smaller rooms, a 2,300-square meter exhibition space, a banquet facility that can accommodate 1,000 people, and parking facility that can accommodate 300 automobiles. In addition, the Centro also offers conference interpreting systems (six conference interpreting booths) and audiovisual presentation equipment, including a megascreen, making it an ideal venue for international events. About 65 percent of all hotel guests are conference participants. Hilton's sales offices in Italy (Milan) and overseas (in Germany, the United Kingdom, France, Sweden, and the Emirate of Dubai) are responsible for conference sales.

Tour operators constitute a second target group, accounting for 25 percent of the hotel's business. Their demand is highest in the months of July and August, when demand exceeds supply—Sorrento's location on the Bay and up a steep hill does not allow for space that could accommodate additional hotels. Only 10 percent of the hotel's business comes from individual bookings, Internet, and telephone.

Sorrento Palace's main target market is Italy. In addition, the hotel also actively targets groups from the United Kingdom, Germany, Belgium, France, and Japan—in that order, according to Mr. Tantawi. Visitors from the United States constituted an important presence at the hotel, particularly in the summer, in organized tours; however, after the terrorist attacks of September 11, 2001, demand has fallen sharply.

Mr. Tantawi would like to direct the hotel's marketing strategies to the United States. In particular, he would like to increase conference attendance at the hotel, as well as the number of tour groups and individual tourists in the off-season (November to March). At present, the hotel draws guests primarily from Italy and the United Kingdom. However, because European economies tend to follow a similar cycle, it is preferable for the hotel to diversify to other markets. Recently, the hotel has made extensive marketing attempts aimed at Japanese tour groups, with great success. Mr. Tantawi would like to find a way to bring in more tourists from the United States—especially conferences and tour groups.

E-2 Marketing Strategies

Discussion Questions

1. How should Hilton Sorrento Palace market more effectively to the U.S. market? Design marketing communication strategies aimed at consumers in the United States promoting the differentiating characteristics of the hotel—views, restaurants, pools, etc. Share your solutions in class and e-mail them to dbd_sorrento@hilton.com.

2. An important difference between the Hilton Sorrento Palace and other Hilton and competing hospitality properties is the reliance on the conference segment. How should the hotel market more effectively to other market segments—in particular, individual guests and their families?

Note

1. Interview with Mr. Ziad Tantawi, Director of Business Development.

F

AvtoVAZ: Maintaining Local Competitive Advantage

Dana Lascu, Maria Vornovitsky,
and Ramil Zeliatdinov

Avto VAZ, or Automobile Factory of the Volga Region, also known as VAZ, was created in 1966 by the Soviet government. The government had as a goal to create a venue for the mass production of affordable automobiles for the Soviet consumer. The company was built by transplanting a defunct Fiat assembly plant from Italy to Togliatti, a small industrial town on the Volga River shores.

F-1 AvtoVAZ in the Soviet Era

AvtoVAZ's first car, the Zhiguli (better known in the West as Lada), was built based on Fiat 124, an automobile produced in Italy twenty years earlier. This first Lada was produced on April 19, 1970, and quickly became Russia's most popular passenger automobile.[1] Its first model was VAZ 2101, which was endearingly called "kopeika" (the penny). It was considered to be of very high quality, and many of these models can still be seen on the road today. Russians were so infatuated with this automobile that there was a movie made titled *Kopeika*, dedicated to this automobile, illustrating the life of the car and its owners.

Over the years, the factory began to gain popularity as it strove to "supply Russian citizens with cars especially made for the tough Russian climate and harsh road conditions."[2] During the Soviet era, AvtoVAZ quickly grew and expanded its production of the Lada. It later introduced Niva, a new model, in 1977, and Samara, in the 1980s. These efforts allowed the company to move ahead of other Soviet automobile manufacturers AZLK, producer of Moskvich, a higher-end automobile, and AvtoGAZ, producer of the Volga, an automobile used primarily for government officials and functions.

F-2 Post-Soviet AvtoVAZ

After 1989, the end of Communism brought drastic changes to the political and economic environment. In addition to the breakup of the Soviet Union, the drive toward a new market economy placed substantial pressure on the old state-owned enterprises. AvtoVAZ needed to implement important changes in order to continue to compete in the new transition economy and to operate successfully in an unstable economic environment. The company privatized immediately after the fall of Communism—it was the first automobile company in Post-Soviet Russia to adapt to a market environment[3]—and promptly lost its former government protection. It also became a target of corruption and mismanagement. At first, the Yeltsin government turned a blind eye to conflicts of interest and theft by corporate managers to win support for policies such as privatization. Today, Russia and AvtoVAZ are paying the price: Companies are held hostage by networks that rob the government of tax revenues, soak up cash needed for industrial modernization, and fuel organized crime.[4]

In 1989, Boris A. Berezovsky, a management-systems consultant to AvtoVAZ, organized a nationwide car-dealership chain that would later bring him vast wealth; he persuaded AvtoVAZ Chief Executive Vladimir Kadannikov to supply him with automobiles without up-front payment. As hyperinflation raged in the early 1990s, Berezovsky earned billions of rubles, partly by delaying payments for AvtoVAZ cars.[5] When the company privatized, in 1993,[6] Kadannikov and Berezovsky set up a company, called the All-Russian Automobile Alliance, which gradually amassed a 34 percent stake in AvtoVAZ. Other AvtoVAZ managers and employees own 35 percent of the company, and Automotive Finance Corp., an affiliate headed by Kadannikov, holds an estimated 19 percent.[7]

Subsequently, trading companies mushroomed around AvtoVAZ, taking advantage of its need for parts and its poor distribution network. The companies swapped components for cars—straight from the factory—at prices as much as 30 percent below market value. Many traders took cars without prepaying, often waiting months before settling. By late 1996, some 300 trading companies were operating with AvtoVAZ. While they raked in millions of dollars in profits, they also owed AvtoVAZ $1.2 billion, about 35 percent of annual sales, for cars delivered to dealers.[8] Furthermore, organized crime became involved in AvtoVAZ, requiring payments equivalent to $100 per automobile to ensure safe delivery. The late 1990s, however, announced a new period for AvtoVAZ, one in which the company was forced to address these irregularities. These changes, along with a slowdown in rampant inflation, have helped the company turn around and have enabled it to explore new growth options through joint ventures.

F-3 AvtoVAZ Today

Currently, AvtoVAZ has a substantial part of the Russian automobile market. A high percentage of automobiles on Russian roads (70.31 percent, or 960,000 automobiles) are produced by AvtoVAZ, while only 13.02 percent are produced by its largest Russian competitor, AvtoGAZ. In provincial Russia, there are primarily just two makes of automobiles: the Zhiguli, by AvtoVAZ, which has about 60 percent of the market share, and the Volga, by AvtoGAZ.[9] AvtoVAZ exports more than 98,000 automobiles yearly.[10]

Even though AvtoVAZ operates less efficiently than its foreign competitors (it builds an automobile in 320 hours, whereas it takes an average of 28 hours to build an automobile at a European plant[11]), it is a perfect fit with the budget and aptitudes of the Russian consumer. AvtoVAZ touts itself as "optimal for the Russian market relationship between price and quality."[12]

Indeed, Russian automobile buyers spend an average price of $5,000 to $6,000 for a new Lada and have an interesting relationship to the automobile. For example, VAZ owners hardly ever use official dealer automobile services; instead, they prefer to use private garages, with self-taught mechanics. Russian automobile buyers are practical: They do not expect the automobile to function perfectly right off the assembly line; the automobile's performance problems are addressed by the private garages at a reasonable fee. Russians expect their brand new Ladas to have some sort of defect; it is recommended to take the car for tuning as soon as it is bought. The tuning typically consists of a complete change of transmission, some modification of the battery, and a complete change of brakes and tires.[13]

Russian buyers are not too concerned about design—their main consideration is price. Russians also make practical choices when it comes to automobile options: They prefer metallic color, which lasts longer; metal protection for the bottom against winter damage; and rubber mats so that they do not vacuum the automobile often. Russian drivers value Ladas for their simplicity, which allows them to fix the automobile themselves; for their durability in withstanding tough climate and road conditions; and for their small size, which makes driving and parking in cities easier.[14]

AvtoVAZ is also planning to introduce a new model, the Kalina, a cheaper car than the Lada; it will sell for about $4,000. However, the company has had difficulty raising the funds to develop the new car.[15]

F-4 VAZ Competitors

In spite of the popularity of its Lada model, AvtoVAZ is rapidly losing market share to foreign competitors. Used automobiles from Europe, especially from Germany, compete directly with the VAZ automobiles, and especially with its latest models—2110, 2111, 2112; German automobiles continue to function without needing any repairs after four years of operation. In fact, without duties on imports of up to 100 percent, Russian automakers would be out of business. Even with the duties, more than 400,000 automobiles are imported yearly.[16] But important drawbacks for imported foreign cars are parts, which are expensive, and service; moreover, neither exists outside Moscow and St. Petersburg.[17]

Competitors such as Daewoo Corporation (Korea) and Skoda (Czech Republic) are also assembling cars in Russia,[18] creating additional competition for AvtoVAZ. General Motors and Ford are trying to set up assembly operations: GM to make 50,000 Chevy Blazers a year in Tatarstan, 700 miles from Moscow, and Ford to assemble 6,000 cars and vans near Minsk.[19]

Among Russian competitors, the worst of the local carmakers, AZLK (making the Moskvich) and truckmaker ZIL, are practically shut down. The viable Russian competitors, truckmaker Kamaz and GAZ, have seen production pick up in the past few years. The GAZ (Gorky Auto Works) factory complex was built in Gorky—known today as Nizhny Novgorod—in the 1930s, with help from Henry Ford. GAZ has a huge plant, with a capacity for 400,000-plus vehicles, including 300,000 medium-size trucks targeted to the military, agriculture, and industrial markets. GAZ has also created a light truck, the Gazelle, targeted toward Russia's new small businesses. The GAZ passenger car is the Volga, targeted initially for government use, which maintains its 1970s looks.[20] As the company is changing its focus from production to profits as its principle, the price of the Volga has been raised, which ultimately has hurt sales (its price is now close to that of many foreign automobiles); consequently, spare capacity was switched to making the more profitable light trucks and minibuses.[21]

Soviet planners decided to build the largest truck factory in the world: They built the Kamaz plant along the Kama River in Tatarstan, near the Urals. Kamaz covers 50 square kilometers with foundries, an engine plant, and an assembly line theoretically capable of producing 150,000 big trucks a year. (For comparison, the U.S. heavy truck market is about 150,000 in a normal year.) The fall of Communism led to a plummeting production, and the company was ripe for restructuring; costs were cut so that Kamaz would produce just 25,000 to 35,000 units a year, and the firm Deloitte & Touche was hired to keep the books and suggest improvements. The firm Kohlberg Kravis Roberts agreed to raise $3.5 billion over six years in exchange for 49 percent of Kamaz; the money was used to develop a new 25-ton truck for the oil and timber industries—a tractor trailer capable of competing with the best from abroad, with a diesel engine from Cummins (of the U.S.), a transmission from ZF (of Germany), and a cab from DAF (of the Netherlands)—and a light truck to challenge the Gazelle. Kamaz is also moving into passenger cars, with a microcar, the 30hp Oka, which sells for $3,500. Kamaz loses $1,000 or so per automobile, but its goal is to be profitable at 50,000 units.[22]

The last of the still-healthy Russian carmakers is UAZ. It makes off-road utility vehicles and small buses, for a total of 93,000 yearly. Its designs date back to the 1970s. The company has limited working capital.[23]

F-5 The AvtoVAZ–GM Joint Venture

General Motors and the European Bank for Reconstruction and Development, whose mission is to finance economic development projects in Eastern Europe, have created a new opportunity for AvtoVAZ: a $340 million joint venture to manufacture off-road vehicles in Togliatti. GM owns a 41.5 percent stake in the joint venture and invested $100 million; EBRD has a 17 percent stake, with $40 million, lending an additional $100 million; and AvtoVAZ contributed manufacturing facilities and intellectual property valued at $100 million, for a 41.5 percent stake. The new company produces the new GM-branded Niva, aiming for a maximum yearly output of 75,000 vehicles, of which more than half are built for export.[24] The new Niva is sold in Western Europe and to markets in Africa, Asia, Latin America, and the Middle East, where the old Niva was popular.[25] In Germany, the Niva will be equipped with engines from Adam Opel.[26]

The joint venture is attempting to maintain the price of the new cars below $10,000 (still beyond the reach of most Russian automobile buyers), but this requires dependence on domestic components; and lack of these in sufficient volumes and at required quality levels have previously set back plans by Ford (U.S.) and Fiat (Italy) to produce for the Russian market.[27]

The Niva sport-utility vehicle looks very attractive and has an impressive design. However, Russian consumers, in addition to balking at its price, still perceive it as being of lower quality: The automobile is assembled on the VAZ platform by VAZ workers. Also, the automobile body is produced at VAZ facilities—not at new GM facilities—so the Niva buyers do not expect the automobile finishing to be superior and last longer than that of the Niva ancestor, VAZ 21213.

Discussion Questions

1. Discuss the positioning strategies of the different competitors in the Russian market. Are the competitors competing for the same segments? Explain.

2. Address the potential contribution of the GM–AvtoVAZ joint venture to creating competitive advantage for the AvtoVAZ.

Notes

1. www.vaz.ru
2. www.vaz.ru
3. www.vaz.ru
4. Carol Matlack, "Anatomy of a Russian Wreck," *Business Week*, September 7, 1998, No. 3594, p. 86b.
5. Ibid.
6. www.vaz.ru
7. Matlack, "Anatomy of a Russian Wreck," p. 86b.
8. Ibid.
9. Ben Aris, "A Tale of Two Car Companies," *Euromoney*, January 2002, Vol. 393, pp. 24–25.
10. *Manufacturing Engineering*, "GM's Russian Partner," February 2001, Volume 126, No. 2, pp. 20–22.
11. Matlack, "Anatomy of a Russian Wreck," p. 86b.
12. www.vaz.ru
13. www.avtoreview.ru
14. www.avtoreview.ru
15. Aris, "A Tale of Two Car Companies," pp. 24–25.
16. Jerry Flint and Paul Klebnikov, "Would You Want to Drive a Lada?" *Forbes*, August 26, 1996, Vol. 158, No. 5, p. 66.
17. Ibid.
18. Matlack, "Anatomy of a Russian Wreck," p. 86b.
19. Flint and Klebnikov, "Would You Want to Drive a Lada?" p. 66.
20. Ibid.
21. Aris, "A Tale of Two Car Companies," pp. 24–25.
22. Flint and Klebnikov, "Would You Want to Drive a Lada?" p. 66.
23. Ibid.
24. *Country Monitor*, "GM Seals AvtoVAZ Deal," July 16, 2001, Vol. 9, No. 27, p. 8.
25. *Manufacturing Engineering*, "GM's Russian Partner," February 2001, Vol. 126, No. 2, pp. 20–22.
26. *Country Monitor*, "GM Seals AvtoVAZ Deal," p. 8.
27. ———, "Auto Investment," February 19, 2001, Vol. 9, No. 6, p. 2.

Disneyland Resort Paris: Reinventing the Mouse for the European Market

Dana Lascu and Jessica DiTommaso

Disneyland Resort Paris was known as Euro Disney in its first incarnation on the European continent. After its launch in April 1992, many name changes were made with the purpose of distancing the company from bad publicity.[1] After four different name revisions, the Disney Corporation has settled on Disneyland Resort Paris.

The idea of expanding the Disney magic to Europe proved to be a project that involved more attention to marketing than even this advertising giant could handle. Many Europeans did not want the American dreamland to distract their children, economy, and country from their own home-grown successful entertainment. David Koenig, author of *Mouse Tales: A Behind-the-Ears Look at Disneyland*, commented, "To the Parisian intellectuals, Disneyland was a symbol of everything contemptible about America: artificial, unstimulating, crass, crude, for the masses. Yet here was a 5,000-acre Disneyland springing up half an hour from the Louvre."[2]

From the very beginning, the Disney Corporation had the best of intentions for its European operation. After a successful opening of Disneyland Tokyo, the company was ready for its next international challenge. The company believed that locating the theme park in close proximity to Paris, France, would both ensure growth for Disney and offer an opportunity for it to incorporate different European cultures. It envisioned a Discoveryland that incorporated the histories of European countries through its fairytales: Italy for Pinocchio, England for Alice in Wonderland, and France for Sleeping Beauty's chateau.[3]

As Euro Disney, the company failed in many aspects of its marketing strategy:

- Euro Disney failed to target the many different tastes and preferences of a new continent of more than 300 million people; addressing the needs for visitors from dissimilar countries, such as Norway, Denmark, Germany, on one hand, and Spain, Italy, and France, on the other, was a challenge.
- Disney's high admission costs were 30 percent higher than a Disney World ticket in the United States, and the company refused to offer discounts for winter admissions.
- Euro Disney ignored travel lifestyles of Europeans: Europeans are accustomed to taking a few long vacations, rather than short trips, which would fit with the Disney model.[4] The company also neglected to consider national holidays and traditional breaks when Europeans are more likely to travel.
- Its restaurants did not appeal to visitors. Morris Nathanson Design in Rhode Island was responsible for designing the restaurants for Euro Disney. The company designed classic American-style restaurants— American-style restaurants are considered by most Europeans as exotic and unusual; unfortunately, the Europeans did not respond well to this format.[5]
- Euro Disney assumed that all Europeans wanted gourmet meals, which is not the case. While French consumers tend to live a more lavish lifestyle and spend larger amounts for gourmet meals, many other consumers in Europe do not—especially when they have to also spend large amounts on air travel, resorts, and park entrance fees. Meal scheduling was also problematic: the French, for example, are accustomed to having all businesses close down at 12:30 for meal times, but the park's restaurants were not made to accommodate such larger influxes for meals, leading to long lines

and frustrated visitors.[6] Finally, Euro Disney initially had an alcohol-free policy, which did not fit with local traditions, where wine is an important part of the culture.

Disney's failed marketing strategy for Euro Disney led to below-average attendance levels and product sales; the park was on the edge of bankruptcy in 1994, with a loss per year of more than a billion dollars.[7] Changing strategies—as well as its name, to Disneyland Resort Paris—has recently led to increased revenues of more than 4 percent, with operating revenues increasing by $32 million to $789 million.[8] Net losses have also decreased from $35.4 million to $27.6 million.[9]

With a full-scale change in the company's marketing direction, Disneyland Resort Paris has been successful in attracting visitors from many countries. Access was a priority for Disney. The company worked on access to the park via the fast train—the TGV; it also worked deals with the EuroStar and Le Shuttle train companies.[10] Disney has worked deals with trains and airlines to reduce prices—a move that ultimately benefited all; the price for transportation to Disney has dropped by 22 percent since the park's opening.[11] In 1992, the Walt Disney Company negotiated with Air France to make Air France the "official" Euro Disney carrier. [12] For visitors from the United Kingdom, British Airways is the preferred carrier of Disneyland Resort, and British Airways Holidays, its tour subsidiary, is the preferred travel partner.[13]

Disney also adapted targeting strategies to individual markets to address the interests and values of different segments of European consumers. It placed representatives around the world with the task of researching specific groups of consumers and creating the best package deals for potential visitors; the new Disney offices were established in London, Frankfurt, Milan, Brussels, Amsterdam, and Madrid.[14] Research results led to the tailoring of package deals that were in line with vacation lifestyles of the different European segments. In addition to the package deals, Disney offered discounts for the winter months and half-price discounts for individuals going to the park after 5:00 P.M.

To better accommodate its guests, Disneyland Paris revised its stringent no-alcohol policy, allowing wine and beer to be served at its restaurants. The resort hotels also lowered their room rates and offered less expensive menu choices in their restaurants.[15] The restaurants created more suitable food options, catering to different regional European tastes, but continued to offer large American-size portions.[16] Crepes and waffles are on the menu of almost every street stand in the park.

Mickey Mouse and Donald Duck have French accents, and many rides were renamed to appeal to French visitors: in Adventureland, Le Ventre de la Terre (Galleries under the tree), l'Ile au Tresor (Treasure Island), La Cabane des Robinson (Robinsons' Cabin); in Fantasyland, Le Chateau de la Belle au Bois Dormant (Sleeping Beauty's Castle, rather than Cinderella's Castle at Disney World, United States), Blanche-Neige et les Sept Nains (Snow White and the Seven Dwarfs), Le Carrousel de Lancelot, Le Pays des Contes des Fee (the Country of Fairytales); and in Discoveryland, L'Arcade des Visionnaires, Le Visionarium (a time-travel adventure with Jules Verne), Les Mysteres du Nautilus (Nautilus's Mysteries).

The French-named attractions exist alongside attractions such as Main Street U.S.A., with its Main Street Station, vehicles and horse-drawn streetcars, and Frontierland, with Thunder Mesa River Boat Landing, Legends of the Wild West, Rustler Roundup Shootin' Gallery, and other similar themes. The hotels also have more traditional American themes—New York, Newport Bay, and Sequoia Lodge.

The park also has numerous attractions that appeal to European guests in general, such as Pinocchio's Fantastic Journey, and Cinemas Gaumont, which feature live concerts with performers from around the world.

Along with creating an environment of greater appeal to European visitors, Disney changed the name of its resort to Disneyland Resort Paris. In its advertising strategy, the company decided to focus its efforts on brand building, initially targeting consumers with a new communication strategy implemented by Ogilvy & Mather Direct.[17] Disney changed its advertising, aiming its message at Europeans who did not grow up with Mickey Mouse; in the park's new commercials, parents and grandparents are shown delighting in the happiness of their children and grandchildren. The advertisements feature "children impatient to depart for and thrilled to arrive at the Magic Kingdom or a grandfather delighted by his grand-daughter's excitement at the prospect of seeing Mickey; or grown-ups sitting tensely before riding on the Space Mountain."[18]

The park is also working with Red Cell, a leading Paris-based advertising agency, for all its television campaigns for the park's new attractions.[19]

Disney is capitalizing on its recent European success by offering yet another grand theme park adjacent to Disneyland—the Walt Disney Studios. Disney is attempting to promote Walt Disney Studios in a manner that would not cannibalize attendance at Disneyland Paris.[20] Among its attractions are a Rock'N'Roller Coaster Starring Aerosmith, capitalizing on the U.S. band's success in Europe; Animagique; and Cinemagique. The park is dedicated to the art of cinema, animation, and television, and it focuses on the efforts of many Europeans who made it all possible to bring fantasy to reality.

Discussion Questions

1. How do the values and lifestyles of European consumers differ from those of consumers in the United States? Discuss the Disney failure to address European consumers' preferences based on the respective values and lifestyles.

2. A large proportion of the park's visitors come from Spain and Latin America. How can Disneyland Resort Paris appeal more effectively to this market? Design a new target marketing strategy aimed at the Spanish and Latin American market.

Notes

1. Harriet Marsh, "Variations on a Theme Park," *Marketing*, London, May 2, 1996.
2. David Koenig, *Mouse Tales: A Behind-the-Ears Look at Disneyland*. Irvine: Bonaventure Press, 1994.
3. Ibid.
4. "Euro Disneyland SCA," International Directory of Company Histories, Vol. 20, pp. 209–212.
5. Gail Ghetia, "As American as French fries: Euro Disneyland, when it opens, will feature typically American restaurants," *Restaurant Hospitality*, August 1990.
6. "Euro Disneyland SCA," pp. 209–212.
7. "The Kingdom inside a Republic," *The Economist*, April 13, 1996.
8. Juliana Koranteng, "Euro Disney revenues rise," *Amusement Business*. August 6, 2001.
9. ——— , "Future may be bright for Euro Disney," *Amusement Business*, May 21, 2001.
10. "Euro Disneyland SCA," pp. 209–212.
11. Marsh, "Variations on a Theme Park."
12. Ibid.
13. Barbara J. Mays, "French park still negotiating for airline partnership," *Travel Weekly*, April 20, 1992.
14. "The Kingdom inside a Republic," *The Economist*.
15. Barbara Rudolph, "Monsieur Mickey: Euro Disneyland is on schedule, but with a distinct French accent," *Time*, March 25, 1991.
16. Ibid.
17. Marsh, "Variations on a Theme Park."
18. "The Kingdom inside a Republic," *The Economist*.
19. Juliana Koranteng, "Taking it to the tube: Parc Asterix to unleash national TV campaign," *Amusement Business*, February 11, 2002.
20. Koranteng, "Euro Disney revenues rise."

So, Who's the Target Market Here

Jay Lindquist

H-1 So, Who's the Target Market Here

There are times when we see a print advertisement or watch a television commercial and feel that it could be targeted to more than one market segment. In fact if it weren't for the magazine in which we find the ad or the television program in which the commercial is run we might be hard pressed to get the fit.

Discussion Questions

Let's look at two different print ads, the Exhibit 13-4 Skechers' example and the Gillette Mach3 razor example that is Exhibit 14-7.

1. How could each of these ads be viewed as targeted on a lifestyle, subculture, social class, and reference group? In each case identify the specific lifestyle, subculture, social class and reference group segment you think is being targeted. Then give your rationale. The result should be four separate discussions for each ad.

2. Different individuals will likely come to different conclusions on the target segments. That's fine. What are your ideas?

Enhancing the Quality of Life of the Elderly

M. Joseph Sirgy

I-1 Enhancing the Quality of Life of the Elderly

Professor Joseph Coughlin of the AgeLab at MIT is a professor of management and specializes in developing products and services catering to the elderly. AgeLab is a partnership between MIT, industry, and the aging community. Its mission is to engineer innovative solutions of problems that can enhance the quality of life of the elderly. For example, scientists at AgeLab are developing a lightweight "space suit" for the elderly that can monitor their health and help them move without walkers. The space suit is also designed to protect them from falling by cushioning their fall impact. But one wonders why would the elderly be interested in buying a space suit? Professor Coughlin argues that the baby boomers are now turning elderly. One estimate puts the size of this market at 78 million consumers. Compared to its predecessor, the baby boomer generation grew up with high tech products and services. Therefore, a space suit is likely to appeal to the baby boomer generation turned elderly. This is a good example of developing products and services as a direct function of understanding the needs and motives of target consumers (*American Demographics* 2002[1]).

Another example of developing products and services designed to enhance the quality of life of the elderly is public transportation services. The baby boomer generation grew accustomed to driving their own vehicles. But what happens when they can no longer drive? Will they turn to public transportation? If so, is the public transportation system available in the towns and cities they reside adequate for their needs? How do business marketers and public officials in the many communities throughout the U.S. address this demand? Professor Coughlin believes that transportation is the No. 1 problem that should be addressed with a sense of urgency. The challenge is to provide an alternative solution to the car, especially in the suburbs. The vast majority of people (and yes the baby boomers) live in the suburbs and rural areas. Suburbs and rural areas typically do not have public transportation services. One solution is a regional shuttle service. Elderly baby boomers would call this service from their cell phones, personal digital assistants, or cable TV, and have that vehicle pick them up in half an hour. Providing a reliable shuttle service is very important for the elderly, especially elderly baby boomers used to being very active. Today, many older adults have to book a ride 24 hours in advance. Today's van service for the elderly is not reliable. Professor Coughlin estimates that there is a 1 in 5 chance that the van won't show up. This kind of service makes today's elderly feel hostage in their own homes. Going out for a cup of coffee or to visit a friend is a major undertaking full of risks and pains.

Consider another problem of falling down and needing assistance. Or perhaps the assistance may be related to other reasons. Today's elderly live with others or in assisted-living communities because they know they can count on others being around when and if they need physical assistance. Professor Coughlin envisions a more comprehensive personal emergency response systems. The elderly needing assistance can click on a pendant or wristwatch that taps into a support system. The support system may involve a virtual service collaborators that brings service providers together in a network that may use the Internet as a base. This system would allow companies to offer all kinds of services to the elderly, not only emergency physical assistance but also nutrition with health monitoring, food shopping, among others.

What about shopping at the grocery store and needing to select food items that may not exacerbate health problems such as blood pressure, diabetes, and other disease common to the elderly? Can the elderly shop with devices that can assist them in identifying food items that may not adversely affect their health condition? The problems are many, but so are possible solutions. These solutions can be marketed to the elderly by businesses whose mission is to enhance the quality of life of the elderly. For more information about AgeLab and its research go to the following website: http://web.mit.edu/agelab

Discussion Questions

1. The AgeLab caters to a particular consumer segment—the aging Baby Boomers. What kind of market segment is this? Read the Segmentation part in Chapter 3 and discuss.

2. Product development in the AgeLab is guided by the concept of Quality-of-Life Marketing. Read about this concept in Chapter 17 and describe this concept in some detail. Compare and contrast AgeLab's approach to product development with the traditional marketing approach.

3. Describe the types of innovations launched by the AgeLab from a diffusion-of-innovations perspective (refer to the Diffusion of Innovations part in Chapter 18). Can you predict the rate of diffusion for each of AgeLab's innovations?

4. Develop an ad campaign for each of AgeLab's innovations. Make sure to read Chapter 10 on Communication and Persuasion to help you with this task. Identify the demographic profile of the target market for each innovation. Specify communication goals using the hierarchy-of-effects models. What source factors would you suggest should be used in the communication campaign? Make a recommendation concerning message content, form, context, and execution. Recommend a media schedule too.

Note

1. American Demographics (2002). "Futurespeak: Science's Potential to Create New Markets," *American Demographics* (May issue), p. 49.

The Diffusion of E-mail in Health Care

M. Joseph Sirgy

J-1 The Diffusion of E-mail in Health Care

E-mail is actually a recent phenomenon. Ten years ago people didn't use e-mail. Now e-mail has been diffused quite rapidly into society. Nowadays, business people communicate regularly by e-mail; students e-mail their teachers; consumers gather information about products and services by contacting companies directly by e-mail. But what about e-mail communication between patients and physicians? The diffusion of e-mail communication between patients and physicians has not been as rapid as in other sectors of society. Physicians remain reluctant to some extent.

American Demographics (www.demographics.com) reported the results of a survey released in April by Rochester, N.Y.-based Harris Interactive, shows that about 90 of the patients that have Internet access would like to interact with their doctors online (Fetto 2002[1]). The survey was based on a sample of 2,014 adults. The majority of the patients surveyed indicated that they would be interested in using e-mail to ask their doctors questions when an office visit isn't necessary (77 percent), to make appointments (71 percent), to refill prescriptions (71 percent), and to retrieve test results (70 percent). Patients are even willing to pay to communicate with their physicians by e-mail. Specifically, 37 percent are willing to pay an average of $10.60 a month, out-of-pocket, or $6.90 per e-mail, for the opportunity to communicate with their doctors by e-mail.

With respect to the physicians, they seem to be cool to that idea. A separate survey of 1,200 U.S. physicians (survey conducted by Deloitte Research and Fulcrum Analytics and reported by Fetto 2002) found that most physicians expect to be reimbursed an average of $57 for a 15-minute e-consultation. Around 23 percent of the physicians indicated that they interact with their patients by e-mail. Of those who are not currently e-mailing, 54 percent said that they may be willing to do so if insurance companies would reimburse them for it; 43 percent indicated that they would do it if they reallocated staff; 42 percent said they would do it if they are presented with proof that e-mail would save time; 37 percent indicated interest if e-mail would help them see more patients; and 37 percent would try it if it can be demonstrated that e-mail can help cut expenses.

Discussion Questions

1. Can you predict the rate of diffusion of e-mail in health care, particularly in relation to the use of e-mail by physicians to communicate with their patients and vice versa? Read the section on Diffusion of Innovations in Chapter 18 and discuss.

2. Describe some of the factors that may facilitate or hinder the diffusion of e-mail between physicians and patients. Read the section on Diffusion of Innovations in Chapter 18 and discuss.

3. If you were a healthcare administrator in a large health corporation that oversees many medical facilities and hospitals in a large metropolitan area, and you know that getting physicians in your healthcare network to use e-mail to communicate with their patients is likely to enhance patient satisfaction, how would you go about persuading the physicians in the network to use e-mail? Read the chapter on Communication and Persuasion (Chapter 10) and discuss.

Note

1. Fetto, John (2002). "Virtual Docs," *American Demographics* (July/August), p. 16.

Streaming Media
Is Catching On

M. Joseph Sirgy

K-1 Streaming Media Is Catching On

For many old timers, the idea of listening to music or watching a video movie on the Internet is alien. However, to a vast majority of the younger generation, this is a common pasttime. This is called "streaming media" for those of us who didn't know. Now, streaming media is catching on quickly with the diffusion of high-speed broadband Internet connections at home. Adults are now beginning to use streaming media in the same ways teenagers have done for a while.

Leslie O'Shea, a writer for *American Demographics* (www.demographics.com), has reported that in 2002 about 80 million Americans say they have listened to streaming audio or watched streaming video over the Internet, up from 61 million in 2001 (O'Shea 2002[1]). The figures are based on a report released in February 2002 by New York-based Arbitron (www.arbitron.com), an international media research firm, and Sommerville, N.J.-based Edison Media Research. In 2000, Arbitron found that 39 percent of teens and 35 percent of 18- to 24-year-olds have used streaming media compared to 23 percent of 45- to 54-year-olds and 9 percent of 55- to 64-year-olds. The 2002 Arbitron report shows, with respect to "monthly streamies," that the older group is catching on—younger than 18-year-olds (19 percent), 18- to 24-year-olds (16 percent), 25- to 34-year-olds (21 percent), 45- to 54-year-olds (17 percent).

These studies also show that blacks and Hispanics constitute a growing market for streaming media. Fifty-five percent of black Internet users and 57 percent of Hispanics say that have used streaming media, compared with 48 percent of whites. Streamies are also wealthier at large. The data shows that these people have more discretionary income and buy more products online than Internet users as a whole. Specifically, nearly 50 percent of streamies live in homes with annual incomes exceeding $50,000, compared with 43 percent of all Internet users and just 34 percent of the total U.S. population. Seventy percent of streamies have purchased something online, compared with 56 percent of all Internet users. Streamies also spend more time on the Internet (almost twice as much) than Internet users as a whole.

O'Shea asks the million-dollar question: Will businesses offering audio and video services on the Internet adopt a commercial-free subscription model like HBO or use an advertising and subscription model like AOL?

Discussion Questions

1. Do you have any thoughts about advantages and disadvantages of the two subscription models? Use Diffusion-of-Innovation concepts and models in Chapter 18 to formulate your ideas.
2. Why do think Hispanics and African-American consumers use streaming media more than whites? Formulate your answer based on your understanding of the demographic and consumer profile of these subcultural groups. Read Chapter 13, particularly the section on Subculture Based on Ethnicity.
3. Develop ideas for a communications campaign targeting Hispanics and African-Americans to further stimulate the adoption of streaming media. Read the chapter on Communication and Persuasion (Chapter 10) to help you develop ideas.

Note

1. O'Shea, Leslie (2002). "Mainstreamies: Long Perceived as Strictly for Teens, Streaming Media is Now Growing in Popularity across Most Demographics," *American Demographics* (July/August), pp. 16–17.

Consumer Trends

M. Joseph Sirgy

L-1 Consumer Trends

Pamela Danziger wrote a book entitled "Why People Buy Things They Don't Need" (Danziger 2002[1]) that highlighted several consumer trends. These are:

- Shift from buying things to buying experiences
- Shift to realism and naturalism
- Increasing emphasis on time
- Shift in retail outlet selection

Danziger argues as the Baby Boomers age their needs will change from "things" to "experiences". The majority of the Baby Boomers are going through a "midlife crisis" stage. This transition into maturity gets them to buy services that meet emerging needs. They will begin to face mortality. In doing so, they become motivated to experience aspects of life they never had. Examples include travel, health, personal development, aesthetics, knowledge, languages, and cooking, among others. Services providing these services are likely to prosper, as well as manufacturers of goods related to those experiences. For example, automobile manufacturers focus on providing recreation vehicles that can satisfy the need for adventure for the Baby Boomer generation. The Baby Boomers will experience their second adolescence—their first was during the 1960s when they lashed out against society, against materialism, and established traditions and customs. After lashing out, they got married, settled down, and fell back to the pursuit of material possessions. Now that they have aged, they are ready to exchange their material possessions with adventure. They may travel to China or hike the Appalachian Trail, take a French cooking class, or drive cross country on a Harley.

A second trend involves a shift toward realism and naturalism. Today's world is becoming more digital. The Internet is playing an increasingly important role in people's lives. Reality is becoming "virtual." Cyberspace is taking over real space. Danziger argues that because of the level of saturation of computers and cyber technologies in our lives, we feel that we need to get back to reality. Reality, in this case, may translate into nature and history. Therefore, people may become increasingly motivated to escape virtual reality and experience natural reality by visiting parks, going on hikes, experiencing nature and wildlife, and visiting historical sites and destinations. People may do more gardening as they try to get closer to nature, build garden pools, and populate their habitats with birds, frogs, and nature's friendly animals and pets.

A third trend is our increasing emphasis on time. We are becoming very conscious of time, how we use it and how we waste it. We realize we have a finite amount of time to do things, especially the kinds of things we like to do. We are becoming acutely aware of our aging process and impending mortality. Therefore, according to Danziger, we seek to allocate time wisely to get much more out of life. This translates into seeking products and services that are time-efficient. To save time, consumers increasingly shop at mega stores. Doing so allows them to save time from shopping so they can spend more time on other more pleasurable activities. Consumer will do more shopping per shopping trip to save time too. They will turn to the Internet for shopping because Internet shopping is more time-efficient.

As a result of consumers emphasizing time-efficient shopping, they will shop less and less at traditional department stores and more at mass merchants, discounters, and warehouse marts. Examples include Wal-mart, Target, Kmart, Costco, and Sam's Club. Non-store retailers (such as catalogers, mail-order marketers, television shopping, direct sales, party-plan marketers, and e-tailers) will experience more business. Danziger also argues that large national specialty chains

(Bed Bath & Beyond, Linen 'n' Things, Pier 1, Pottery Barn, Williams-Sonoma, Restoration Warehouse, Home Depot, Lowe's, and so forth) will increasingly benefit from this trend. Consumers are shopping in these national specialty stores to satisfy their need for high quality "specialty" products. The national specialty chains with their brand equity signal to consumers high quality, and consumers are increasingly flocking to these stores and away from local specialty stores.

Discussion Questions

1. Compare and contrast Danziger's three trends with the discussion of traditional and emergent American values and consumer behavior in Chapter 12.

2. Identify marketing strategies that are logically deduced from Danziger's trends. Compare these marketing strategies from those logically deduced from the discussion of traditional and emergent trends in Chapter 12.

Note

1. Danziger, Pamela N. (2002). Why People Buy Things They Don't Need, Paramount Market Publishing, Inc. (www.paramountbooks.com).

Demographic Trends:
Marketing Implications

M. Joseph Sirgy

M-1 Demographic Trends: Marketing Implications

Peter Francese, the founder of *American Demographics* (www.demographics.com), reported demographic trends that are having significant marketing implications (Francese 2002–03[1]). Francese notes 10 emerging trends:

1.   Aging boomers
2.   Delayed retirement
3.   The changing nature of work
4.   Greater educational attainment—especially among women
5.   Looming labor shortages
6.   Increased immigration
7.   Rising Hispanic influence
8.   Shifting birth trends
9.   Widening geographical differences
10. Changing age structure

Baby boomers turned 55 in 2001. In the next 10 years, this segment will amount to 38 million in the U.S. These consumers will have plenty of money to spend. This is because the baby boomers tend to more educated than their previous cohorts and make more money. Businesses likely to benefit the most include full-service restaurants, travel-related businesses, builders of second homes, and health and fitness businesses.

Baby boomers will also delay retirement. They have done so in relation to getting married and having children. Many will start collecting Social Security benefits at the age of 67 not 65. Delayed retirement can also be attributed to high levels of educational attainment and higher paying professional careers than previous generations.

Workers are likely to continuously invest in education. Past generations consumed educational opportunities only when they were young. Today's and tomorrow's workers will invest in education throughout their careers to enhance their professional development. Therefore educational institutions will benefit from serving this growing market.

In today's and tomorrow's job market, the jobs are changing in terms of physical and intellectual requirements. More jobs require intellectual skills, and less jobs require physical skills. Again, this trend favors those institutions of higher education. More people will enroll in colleges to attain the required intellectual skills for the available jobs. And because women are more equipped to deal with the intellectual than physical demands of many jobs, more job opportunities will be made available to women. This trend points to the fact that women are likely to have more money to spend than their previous generation and certainly more financial independence.

Statistics concerning the labor market show that many service-related industries such as nursing are experiencing labor shortages. To deal with these shortages, many organizations are recruiting foreign workers. This is reflected in increased immigration. Based on the 2000 census, 40 percent of the country's population growth is directly attributed to immigration. The majority of immigrants come from Latin America. This is one of the factors accounting for the increased size of the Hispanic population in the U.S. (estimated at 35 million in 2000). The Hispanic population is expected to grow by 35 percent in the next 10 years. Hispanics typically have larger households, and therefore they spend more money on food, clothing, and other items for children.

More women are having children during their later years (during their late 30s) and many of them have multiple births. This trend of older mothers (who typically are career women with earning power) translates into greater spending for baby-related goods and services. More minority women (Hispanic and African-American women) are having more births than their white counterparts. This means that elementary schools will have to accommodate an increase in minority students in the next decade or so.

The growth in population is occurring in selected geographic regions of the country. Specifically, the growth is concentrated in the south and southwest (Texas, California, and so on). Furthermore, the growth is more evident in suburban areas. More retail outlets will be built in the suburbs as population continues to saturate these areas.

With respect to changing age structure, Peter Francese points to the impact of the 71 million Echo Boomers (8- to 25-year-olds). The Echo Boomers are a demographic force that marketers have to reckon with. This consumer segment is not only large but perhaps very different in their consumption habits, compared with Gen X and Baby Boomer consumers.

Marketers that are savvy enough to understand these demographic trends are likely to position themselves effectively in the marketplace to take advantage of new opportunities as well as counter the threats of evolving demographic patterns. In contrast, failing to anticipate what is coming in the future may cause the demise of many businesses.

Discussion Questions

1. Compare and contrast Francese's 10 demographic trends with the discussion of traditional and emergent American values and consumer behavior in Chapter 12.

2. Identify marketing strategies that are logically deduced from Francese's trends. Compare these marketing strategies from those logically deduced from the discussion of traditional and emergent trends in Chapter 12.

Note

1. Francese, Peter (2002–03). "Top Trends for 2003." *American Demographics* (December 2002/January 2003), pp. 48–51.

Family Values: The Case of the S.C. Johnson Company

M. Joseph Sirgy

N-1 Family Values: The Case of the S.C. Johnson Company

Family values are the kind of values that promote the propagation of families, family nurturance, and healthy communities. Families are said to make up the basic unit of society, not the individual. Social critics argue that many of our social ills (crime, violence, sexual promiscuity, and rampant materialism) are directly and indirectly related to values that promote the individual self over and above the family. Family values are the kind of cultural values that are high on American list of ideal cultural values. Politicians tout themselves as standing up for family values. Churches, synagogues, mosques, temples, and other places of worship lay claim to the notion that family values are at the heart of good society, humanity, and the spiritual life. Companies that position themselves as representing family values are successful in creating an aura of trust and commitment. One such company is the S.C. Johnson Company.

S.C. Johnson, formerly JohnsonWax, is a private, "family company" (http://www.scjohnson.com). It makes and markets a broad array of household goods under the Fantastik, Saran, and Edge brands, among others. S.C. Johnson has run many advertising campaigns such as the Pledge Grab-It mop and Ziploc. One of their ad campaigns touts "family values" in which Johnson (great grandson of the company's founder and chief executive over the period of its great expansion) emphasizes the fact that the company is not only family-owned but also is dedicated to serve the family. He says, "in many ways taking care of one's home is just like taking care of a family, and we've never lost sight of that" (Grimm 2002, p. 47[1]).

Not only does the company emphasize the notion that they are a family company promoting family values in advertising but also in packaging. The company's name is on the package of every product with a tag namely "A Family Company." Reinforcing the customers' image of family company standing up for family values is a good marketing strategy. Grimm (2002) reports that the company's own consumer research showed 80 percent of Americans considered products from family-owned companies trustworthy, versus 43 percent who say the same of those from publicly traded companies. This image breeds trust, which in turn affects customer loyalty and commitment. More recent research conducted by S.C. Johnson showed that 62 percent of surveyed adults said their trust in large family companies has stayed the same during the recent corporate scandals and 21 percent said their trust has decreased. Compare these figures with public companies. The same survey showed that 33 percent said their trust has remained the same for public companies, while 61 percent said it has declined (Grimm 2002).

The moral of this story is that the promise of a good brand is a reflection of the people behind it. Consumers make attributions about the quality of the brand and the company service aspects by their image of the people behind that brand, especially corporate executives. The more they feel they trust these people the more they feel the company products and services are of high quality and can be trusted to deliver on their promises.

Discussion Questions

1. Read the chapter on Culture (Chapter 11) and discuss the S.C. Johnson case from that perspective.
2. Read the discussion pertaining to traditional and emergent American values in Chapter 12. Comment on the effectiveness of S.C. Johnson's advertising campaign.
3. Read Chapter 10 on Communication and Persuasion and comment on the effectiveness of the campaign. What changes would you recommend to enhance the effectiveness of the campaign?

Note

1. Grimm, Matthew (2002). "Voice in the Wilderness." *American Demographics* (October), pp. 46–47.

Socially Responsible Consumers or Green Consumers

M. Joseph Sirgy

O-1 Socially Responsible Consumers or Green Consumers

What does it mean to be a green consumer? Is a green consumer a person that recycles? A consumer that cuts back on driving? A consumer that drives a more fuel-efficient vehicle? A consumer that uses power sources that do not pollute the environment, such as wind and solar energy? All the above? A recent study, commissioned by Austin, Texas-based Green Mountain Energy Company (http://www.greenmountain.com/index.jsp), shows that 44 percent of adults say they would try harder to be green if more environmentally friendly products and services were readily available; and 20 percent said they would do so if they thought their efforts would make a difference (Gardyn 2002[1]). The survey was based on a random sample of 1,018 adult Americans conducted in 2002 by Princeton, N.J.-based Opinion Research Corporation (http://www.opinionresearch.com).

The survey results indicated that the tendency to be green is concentrated among those in the higher income brackets ($50,000+) and those living in households with three or more people. Those in the lower income bracket and living alone or in households with less than three people claim that they may become green consumers if they believe that their efforts would make a difference. This implies that the reason for not being green is driven by a perception of an external locus of control—that is, whatever I do will not make much of a difference. Other reasons for not being green include the belief that green products and services are more difficult and time-consuming to find, and not knowing how to start consuming green products and services (Gardyn 2002).

These reasons for failing to become green should alert public policy makers that socially responsible consumption is a matter of learning. Information and educational green campaigns can make a big difference in teaching consumers to become green, especially those that are mostly motivated, but simply don't know how. In sum, this research clearly shows that social marketing programs can make a difference in enhancing sustainable consumption. The focus of these programs should be educational—educate consumers how to become green.

Discussion Questions

1. Read the chapter on Consumer Behavior and Society (Chapter 17), particularly the section on The Dark Side of the Consumer Society. Do you believe that consumers have an ethical duty to engage in behaviors that sustains the environment for future generations? Discuss.
2. Do you believe that consumer goods companies have an ethical obligation to market goods that are friendly to the environment? Why or why not? Read Chapter 17 on Consumer Behavior and Society—particularly the section on Ethics in Marketing— to help you formulate your answer.
3. Develop ideas for a social marketing campaign dealing with sustainable consumption. Read Chapter 10 on Communication and Persuasion to help you generate good ideas.

Note

1. Gardyn, Rebecca (2002). "Being Green." *American Demographics* (September), pp. 10–11.

I Am Proud to Be American

M. Joseph Sirgy

P-1 I Am Proud to Be American

According to a recent Gallup poll (conducted in June 2002), 65 percent of respondents say that they are "extremely" proud to be American, up from 55 percent in January 2001 (Wellner 2002[1]). This rise of American patriotism has caused marketers to take advantage of this sentiment in their marketing efforts. For example, Sears Portrait Studios introduced a new line of patriotic greeting cards and backgrounds at its 1,000 stores nationwide. GM launched the "Let's Keep America Rolling" campaign immediately after 9/11 (Wellner 2002).

However, consumers are not responding favorably to businesses using patriotic messages, signs, and emblems. According to recent polls conducted by *American Demographics*/Ipsos-Reid polls (conducted into two waves—in 2001 and 2002), most consumers do not endorse the notion that business should focus on contributing to the nation's patriotic spirit through advertising (Wellner 2002). *American Demographics* (www.demographics.com) reporter, Alison Stein Wellner, asks, "If personal levels of patriotism gained strength over the past year, why wasn't there a parallel increase in support for businesses that affiliate themselves with patriotic word and deed?" (Wellner 2002, p. 50). Three explanations. The first explanation may be that Americans' patriotic sentiment has shot up as a direct result of 9/11 and then came back to "normal." The second explanation is the backlash Americans may feel about perceived infringements of civil freedoms. The third explanation is that consumers are becoming numb to flag-waving because so many companies have taken advantage of it (Wellner 2002).

The same surveys also show that women are more likely to be patriotic than men; older people are more patriotic than the young; and the retired and less educated are the most likely to be influenced by patriotic ads. The unemployed are also more likely to support patriotic spirit in advertising (Wellner 2002).

Patriotism also plays an important role in the "buy American products" campaigns. 2002 data from *American Demographics*/Ipsoss-Reid polls (reported in Wellner 2002) show that 69 percent of the respondents say that companies should focus on making it clear that their products are "made in America," up from 64 percent in 2001. However, a much smaller share of consumers (around 7 percent) make purchase based on the belief that the product is made in the U.S.A. This result comes from an online survey of 1,000 American adults conducted in May 2002 by Euro RSCG (reported in Wellner 2002).

These results affirm the fact that consumers purchase decisions are multifaceted and driven by many factors, one being "made in the U.S.A." Marketers should be able to better understand how this decision criterion interacts with other decision criteria in affecting purchase decisions of their target consumers.

Discussion Questions

1. Read the chapter on Culture (Chapter 11) and discuss how cultural value such as American patriotism has changed over the years.
2. Read the discussion pertaining to traditional and emergent American values in Chapter 12. Comment on the effectiveness of marketing communication campaigns in which the focal message is "Made in the U.S.A."
3. Read Chapter 10 on Communication and Persuasion and comment on the effectiveness of the country-of-origin advertising campaigns.

Note

1. Wellner, Alison Stein (2002). "The Perils of Patriotism." *American Demographics* (September), pp. 49–51.

Video-on-Demand:
The Wave of the Future

M. Joseph Sirgy

Q-1 Video-on-Demand: The Wave of the Future

Video-on-demand (VOD) is an interactive media in which consumers can watch selected videos (from a menu) on demand. Instead of having network and cable programmers decide what the audience can watch on TV and when, viewers can choose programs to suit their own needs and schedule. Rather than drive down to the nearest video rental store, VOD allows the consumer to rent their desired movies by clicking their TV sets from their living rooms. Viewers typically have an enabled digital set-top box, which selects and accesses movies listed on the VOD channel. Cable companies update each digital box with their latest offerings. When a viewer chooses a movie, the cable operator's servers stream video into that specific digital cable box.

Subscription to VOD is based on two models. One model is subscription VOD (SVOD) that allows the viewer to watch whatever is available for a basic monthly fee. The other subscription model is standard VOD in which viewers order individual movie titles for a fee (typically $3.95 for a new release and $2.95 for other titles). This model is referred to as "pay-per-view" or "near-video-on-demand" (NVOD) (Paul 2002[1]).

Pamela Paul, a writer at *American Demographics* (www.demographics.com) reports that in 2002, about 2.5 million homes (slightly more than 2 percent of the 105.5 million TV households in the U.S.) were able to receive VOD from their cable company via subscription (Paul 2002). Only one-third of these households (833,000 subscribers) chose to use this service. This figure is up from 300,000 households in 2001. Market forecasts project VOD subscriptions to reach 59.3 million households by the year 2012. This research and forecast data come from research conducted by New York-based research firm Jupiter Media Metrix (http://www.jupiterresearch.com/bin/item.pl/home).

In terms of the demographic profile of VOD users, they seem to be mostly upscale, educated and suburban. They are early adaptors of technological innovations. This profile comes from research conducted by nCUBE, a VOD company (http://www.ncube.com).

What are the barriers to VOD subscriptions? Paul (2002) argues VOD requires digital cable, which has not spread as quickly as hoped for. Estimates are 14 million homes in the U.S. have digital cable. A second barrier seems to be the tough negotiations among cable operators, VOD distributors, and movie studios. Trying to negotiate an outcome that is favorable to all parties concerned has proven to be a difficult task. A third barrier seems to be the number of movie options available to VOD subscribers. Viewers do not have a wide assortment of movies to choose from. One cause is that many releases are tied up in licensing arrangements that do not include VOD.

Discussion Questions

Discussion Questions

1. Can you predict the rate of diffusion of VOD? What factors are likely to facilitate or hinder the diffusion of VOD in the next decade or so? Use the concepts and models in the Diffusion of Innovations part of Chapter 18 to formulate your answer.

2. Which subscription model is likely to accelerate the rate of diffusion of VOD—SVOD vs. NVOD? Use the concepts and models in the Diffusion of Innovations part of Chapter 18 to formulate your answer.

3. How can advertisers use VOD as a new advertising medium? Read the Communication and Persuasion chapter (Chapter 10) to help formulate your answer.

4. How can marketers of VOD reach out to advertisers to convince them to use VOD as an effective advertising medium? Concepts and models from the Organizational Buying part of Chapter 18 may be useful here.

Note

Note

1. Paul, Pamela (2002). "Television Gets Targeted," *American Demographics* (September), pp. 22–26.